CAN
YOUR FOUR-YEAR-OLD
MAKE YOU A HAPPIER, LES...
AND MORE EFFICIENT PARENT?
YOU BET!
FIND OUT ABOUT—

- Embarrassing moments . . . how to deal with a four-year-old's fascination with bowel movements, belly buttons, body parts, and forbidden words—without turning red. *See pages 8, 18, 125–28.*

- Words that will work a miracle . . . what to say to give your child an instant smile, raise self-esteem, and change behavior quicker than criticism. *See page 31.*

- Hyperactivity . . . how to determine if your "always on the go" Four-year-old is truly hyperactive. *See pages 42–44.*

- Kindergarten readiness . . . school too soon can cause lifelong problems, so note this warning for parents of "fall babies." *See page 84.*

- Encouraging creativity . . . fifteen activities you can initiate to stimulate your child's natural talents and have a great time too! *See pages 96–97.*

- Your child's body type: round and plump or bony and angular . . . does it predict behavior, temperament, and social success? *See pages 100–7.*

. . . and more!

YOUR FOUR-YEAR-OLD

"I think [these books] are delightful and likely to capture the imagination of young parents enough to get them through these years. . . . I think the books will be both a pleasure and support for many parents."

—T. Berry Brazelton, M.D., author of
Toddlers and Parents and *Infants and Mothers*

"These are cheerful, optimistic books. . . . I agree with just about everything they say."

—Lendon Smith, M.D., author of
Feed Your Kids Right

Books from the Gesell Institute of Human Development

YOUR ONE-YEAR-OLD
Ames, Ilg, and Haber

YOUR TWO-YEAR-OLD
Ames and Ilg

YOUR THREE-YEAR-OLD
Ames and Ilg

YOUR FOUR-YEAR-OLD
Ames and Ilg

YOUR FIVE-YEAR-OLD
Ames and Ilg

YOUR SIX-YEAR-OLD
Ames and Ilg

YOUR SEVEN-YEAR-OLD
Ames and Haber

YOUR EIGHT-YEAR-OLD
Ames and Haber

YOUR NINE-YEAR-OLD
Ames and Haber

YOUR TEN- TO FOURTEEN-YEAR-OLD
Ames, Ilg, and Baker

your FOUR-YEAR-OLD
Wild and Wonderful

by Louise Bates Ames, Ph.D.,
Frances L. Ilg, M.D.
Gesell Institute of Human Development

Illustrated with photographs

To our daughters,
Joan and Tordis,
and our grandchildren,
Carol, Clifford, Karl and Whittier

A Dell Trade Paperback
Published by
Dell Publishing
a division of
Random House Publishing Group, Inc.
New York, New York

Photo credits appear on page 152.

ISBN 978-0-440-50675-1

Reprinted by arrangement with Delacorte Press

Printed in the United States of America

October 1980

30 29 28 27 26 25

BVG

CONTENTS

chapter one

CHARACTERISTICS
OF THE AGE

The Four-year-old is a funny little fellow, and if you can accept him as such, you will appreciate and enjoy him for what he is. If, on the other hand, you take a sterner stance and feel that his boasting, his swearing, his general expansiveness, and his often out-of-bounds behavior is *wrong*, both you and he may have an unnecessarily hard time of it.

For the most part, we have found the boy or girl of this age to be joyous, exuberant, energetic, ridiculous, untrammeled—ready for anything. What a change he offers as compared to his more difficult, demanding, Three-and-a-half-year-old, just-earlier self! If at times he seems somewhat voluble, boastful, and bossy, it is because it is so exciting for him to enter the fresh fields of self-expression that open up at this wonderful age.

The child at Three-and-a-half characteristically expressed a strong resistance to many things the adult required, possibly because in his own mind the adult was still all-powerful. Four has taken a giant step forward. All of a sudden he discovers that the adult, though still quite powerful, is not *all*-powerful. He now finds much power in himself. He finds that he can do bad things, from his point of view, and the roof does not fall in.

More than this, following its seemingly built-in plan

of interweaving, nature sees to it that whereas the Three-and-a-half-year-old was rather withdrawn and insecure much of the time, Four operates on the expansive and highly sure-of-himself side of life. Four, as Figure 1 shows, is an age when the child is characteristically in a nice state of equilibrium.

Emotional exuberance has its positive as well as its negative side. The typical Four-year-old *loves* adventure, loves excursions, loves excitement, loves *anything* new.

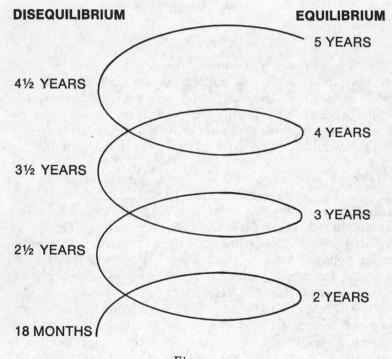

DISEQUILIBRIUM　　　　　　　　　　**EQUILIBRIUM**

5 YEARS

4½ YEARS

4 YEARS

3½ YEARS

3 YEARS

2½ YEARS

2 YEARS

18 MONTHS

Figure 1

Alternation of Ages of Equilibrium and Disequilibrium

He adores new people, new places, new games, new playthings, new books, new activities. No one is more responsive to the adult effort to entertain. He will accept what you have to offer with delightfully uncritical enthusiasm. So, it is a pleasure to provide the child of this age with new toys, books, clothes, experiences, information—because any of these things make his eyes sparkle so, because he is so wholeheartedly appreciative.

In fact, Four *loves* many things, but his emotions tend to be definitely extreme. He loves a lot and he hates a lot. In fact, his hates may be equally as strong as his loves. One can never be quite certain what it will be that will stimulate his hate, but whatever it is, his feeling should be fully respected, at least within reason.

With those children who have a tremendously strong attachment for their mothers (and that is most) there may be especially strong hatred expressed for anything that changes her in the child's eyes. He may hate certain jewelry she wears; he may hate it if she changes her way of wearing her hair. Or, he may especially hate a special look on her face that tells him that she is displeased with him.

He may hate squash, or any other food to which he takes a dislike. Or, he may (alas) hate certain people. He especially hates things that he considers *ugly*, and may at times express a quite remarkable aesthetic sensitivity.

Four loves things that are *new*. The Three-year-old has a conforming mind. Four has a lively mind, and new thoughts and ideas or bits of information may please him as much as do new toys. That is why it is so much fun to talk with him. His incessant "whys" may sometimes pall, but often they lead the way to enthusiastic information-giving on the part of the adult. It is fun to inform some-body who so enthusiastically wishes to be informed.

The key to the Four-year-old's psychology is his high drive combined with his fluid imagination. Four is, indeed, highly versatile. What can he not do? He can be quiet or noisy, calm or assertive, cozy or imperious, suggestible or independent, social, athletic, artistic, literal, fanciful, cooperative, indifferent, inquisitive, forthright, humorous, dogmatic. He is many people in one.

The typical Four-year-old is also speedy. Each thing he does, he does quickly, and he is also speedy as he moves from one interest to the next. For the most part, he does a thing once, and *that's enough*. He isn't interested in perfection; he is interested in getting on to the next activity. Behavior is fluid, and if he does stay with a single activity, that single activity may change so rapidly as to make your head spin.

A good example of the often quite remarkable fluidity of Four's imagination can be seen in his drawing. A Four-year-old in spontaneous drawing may quite typically start with a tree, which turns into a house, which turns into a battleship. Or, even more fluidly, his "person's foot" can grow so large that it develops large toes that turn out to be the back of a bird. And that turns out to be a roller coaster. And that turns out to be the *back* of the roller coaster. (At that point, your Four-year-old may very likely run out of paper.)

Fluidity can be expressed in media other than pencil and paper. For instance, two boys, playing in a sand-pile, decide that they are making volcanoes. However, when it is suggested to them that the volcano's *erupting*, as they had planned, might be too messy, they themselves spout a little and then give up the volcano plan and decide they are digging for dinosaur bones. No bones being forthcoming, they talk awhile about how old dinosaurs get to be (nine thousand years, they think) and then turn their sand into imaginary snow and make snowballs (which do not stick together very well even with the addition of water). So, they turn their snowballs into rotten eggs and say that the last one to talk is a rotten egg. (All this within five minutes of play.)

It is no wonder that adults have to keep on their toes to keep up with speedy, fluid, fanciful Fours. But, fluid as they are, there still remains some of Three's "me-too" quality. If you ask one child in a group what street he lives on, each child in the group then wants to tell where he or she lives, and all may be surprisingly patient and

polite until everyone has had a turn at giving this interesting information.

It may be that Four's expansiveness is sometimes a little too much even for him. At any rate, he likes and respects boundaries and limits, which he does not always

have within himself, and which, therefore, often have to be supplied. In fact, we find that many Fours like very much the verbal restraint of "as far as the tree," "as far as the gate." Others can be reasonably well contained if told, "It's the rule that you do (or do not do) so-and-so."

In fact, many seem to seek for regularity and rules in the happenings around them. Thus, a Four-year-old may come up with the spontaneous conclusion, "It's always so-and-so." This "always" seems to give him security. He may sometimes break the rules, but he likes at least to know what they are.

Also, he sometimes spontaneously restabilizes himself, even in his wilder play. Thus, two boys may pretend they are in a cave (a large pasteboard box) with monsters, but then they protect themselves by pretending that the monsters have disappeared and that they (the boys) are "all safe and sound."

And, for all his expansive and often out-of-bounds tendencies, Four can, when he puts his mind to it, sometimes be very reliable. Many can go on small errands outside the home if these do not involve crossing the street. And many, by Four-and-a-half, have reached the point where they can be trusted to play outdoors without much supervision or checking.

However, when his customary expansiveness combines with his exciting need to see just how far he can go before the grown-ups call a halt, the Four-year-old generously and characteristically very often expresses what we consider the outstanding trait of his age—his love for going out-of-bounds.

A normally vigorous and well-endowed child of this age may seem out of bounds in almost every area of living. Motorwise he not only hits and kicks and spits (if aroused) but may even go so far as to run away from home if things don't please him. Whether he is happy or not, his motor drive is very high. He races up and down stairs, dashes here and there on his trusty tricycle.

Emotionally, too, he tends to be extremely out-of-bounds. He laughs almost too hilariously when things please him; howls and cries more than too loudly when things go wrong. (But he laughs more than he cries, and he loves laughter in others. In fact, he may tell you of his parents, or of other adults, "When they're happy they always laugh." He can, on frequent occasion, be extremely silly.)

But it is his verbally out-of-bounds expressions that are most conspicuous. He exaggerates: "as high as the sky," "ten million bugs," "as big as a house." He boasts: "I have bigger ones at home," "I can do better than that," "My father is stronger than your father." Along with his boasting, he swaggers. Boys like to emphasize their own masculinity by calling each other what they consider to be very masculine names, not their own: "Bill," "Mike," "Joe."

There is much interest in both the products and the process of elimination. Children are especially fascinated by bowel movements. Out for a walk, they may spot every deposit of a dog's bowel movements. Their own buttocks are especially important to them, and when asked what they think with, they may even point to their behinds.

Elimination swearing has its beginning at Four. When angry with a friend, the child may call him an "old poo-poo." In fact, in general, nouns and adjectives tend to be on the unacceptable side, and there is considerable talk about "wee-wee" and "doo-doo." (Even though right in the midst of such a conversation by one child, another may criticize and say, "That's not nice.") There is also much reference to garbage.

This concern about elimination is also seen in the child's great interest in bathrooms, especially in other people's houses. The minute he enters a house, Four may want to see the bathroom. But, though he is much interested in bathrooms and other people's toilet functioning, he tends to be extremely private about his own. He may even go so far as to lock the bathroom door, and many a Four-year-old has locked himself into the bathroom.

And (alas), all too often Four lapses into outright profanity. "Jesus Christ!" is a not-uncommon expletive, even though Four may not fully appreciate what he is saying. When one Four-year-old was heard to repeat the phrase "Goddamn it to Hell!" for each step as he climbed the stairs, his father got the message and became more careful about his own language.

And we have the (supposedly true) story of a little Boston girl whose mother, discouraged by her profanity, told her that if she swore once more, she (the mother) would pack the girl's suitcase and ask her to leave home. The little girl did swear once more. The mother did pack the suitcase and put her and it outside the door. After a few minutes, feeling guilty, the mother went to look for her daughter. The child was still sitting on the steps.

"I thought I told you to leave home," said the mother.

"I would have if I could have thought where the Hell to go," was her daughter's reply.

True or not, this story is all too typical. Or, if not with actual profanity, the child may criticize the adult with epithets and threats: "You're a rat," "I'll sock you." And, not content with unacceptable language, all too often a Four-year-old departs from truth to an extent that any literal-minded adult can label only as outright prevarication. If you meet this, as any other exuberance, with a calm "Is that so?" or with a knowing wink rather than with anger and admonition, he tends to come rather quickly back to reality.

FOUR INTO FIVE

And just in case you are curious about what happens next, here's a word about that interesting transition time —Four into Five.

We know that the typical Four-year-old girl or boy tends to be, as we have told you, extremely exuberant, enthusiastic, outgoing, out-of-bounds. We also know that at Five the same child will in all likelihood be, much of the time, calm, collected, quiet and self-contained, adaptable, conforming, well-adjusted, easy to get on with, happiest and most comfortable while engaged in conservative, close-to-home activities.

How does he get from Four to Five? What is the transition like? Does he all of a sudden one day simply forget his earlier exuberant ways and settle down? Or, is the change more gradual?

It tends to be rather gradual, and sometimes the child

himself seems a bit confused, as if he really does not know whether he is a wild Four-year-old or a calm and quiet Five. At any rate, adults often find his behavior highly unpredictable.

A clue to his own uncertainty is the strong interest of the Four-and-a-half-year-old in whether or not things are "real." Making a drawing of an airplane, he may include a *real* electric cord so that people can plug it in. "Is it real?" is a customary question.

At Four-and-a-half, the child does tend to be a bit more self-motivated than he was just earlier, and he tends to stay on the job better than he did before. Children of this age are much interested in gathering new information, in perfecting old skills. Play is less wild than at Four, and most are better able to stand frustration. But emotions may be quite uncertain, with laughter and tears following each other in quick succession.

And, the child may be less easily shifted than he was just earlier. Some Four-and-a-half-year-olds can be persistently demanding, especially to secure certain objects such as sparklers for the Fourth of July. This kind of demand may be so persistent as to be unacceptable. In fact, when crossed, the child of this age may become obnoxious, sticking out his tongue and making dreadful faces. It may now be less easy to distract him with humor than it was when he was just Four.

At Four-and-a-half, the child is becoming aware of authority, and a new kind of confused but listening expression, mixed with a bit of fear, crosses his face when a parent reprimands him. Parents may like to temper their demands when they see this expression. This may be a time for bargaining.

Now the awareness of "good" and "bad" things begins to dawn. Nothing delights a Four-and-a-half-year-old more than to hear real true stories at bedtime, either about himself or about his parents. He loves stories about how bad his parents were when they were little, and also stories about how good they were.

Prayers, especially spontaneous ones, are welcome at this age and often allay children's bedtime fears. The thought of God the Father, and the thought that He is everywhere, can be comforting to some. Children of this age may like to tell God about their troubles and why they happened. They like to bless all who are near and dear to them or tell God about the people they love.

All in all, the Four-and-a-half-year-old is unpredictable. But if you will keep in mind where the child has been and where he is going, it can help you to define and to understand where he is now.

WARNING!

Here, as at any age, we give you an important warning: *Do not take too seriously what anybody (we included) tells you about how your child will or may behave.*

Child behavior, for all reasonably normal children, does develop in a highly patterned way. Stages of more mature behavior follow those of less mature behavior in a remarkably predictable manner. To a large extent, when we see a child expressing some one certain kind of behavior, we can tell you what will very likely happen next.

We can also, on the basis of having studied thousands of children at every age, give you an estimate of when, *on the average*, your child may be expected to reach each stage.

Almost every child does go through almost all of the stages, and in a rather standard order. What we cannot tell you for sure is *exactly* when your own child will reach each and every stage.

Age norms (our story of what behavior is like at the different ages) are only *averages*. Your child may quite normally be ahead of or behind these averages. So, if we say that a certain behavior is characteristic of Four years of age, and your Four-year-old has not reached this stage yet, you should not feel that you have cause to worry. Your child may be, and quite normally so, a little slower than the average in his development (though the quality of his behavior might be quite superior, indicating that a fine potential will express itself in time.) *Every child has his own timetable. Do not expect that your own child will always perform right on our schedule.*

And then, of course, there are individual differences. Not all Three-year-olds are gentle; not all Four-year-olds are wild.

We tell you about behaviors that are characteristic of the different ages not so that you will check and worry. We tell you what behavior is usually like so that you can, within reason, know what to expect and then *not* worry when your own child's behavior sometimes departs from your ideal.

It is comforting to many parents to know that children do not always behave in a desirable, conforming way; that many perfectly "good" children are often, at some stages, quite normally less than good.

"Now I know he's normal" is what many parents say when they read our often seemingly somewhat lurid descriptions of what behavior can be like at different ages. This is why we write for you—hopefully to prepare you for, and to make you feel comfortable with, the many sometimes rather remarkable ways in which even completely normal children behave as they grow older.

Then you can protect yourself from feelings of guilt, or simple embarrassment, at your child's sometimes unorthodox behavior. Or, you can protect yourself from striking out at your child in an unknowing way or in aroused anger. With knowledge, you can appreciate what the laws of growth are expressing through your child, can smile within yourself at his forms of expression, and can act with confident and loving authority, knowing that this, too, will pass.

chapter two
THE CHILD WITH
OTHER CHILDREN

The typical Four-year-old loves adventure, and other children, for him, can be a big adventure. Especially if they are of his own age they will be, as he is, exciting, active, enthusiastic, out-of-bounds, always ready for something new. And, like him, they will be somewhat unpredictable. This adds spice to playtime.

Children at this age enjoy each other so very much that often playtime goes smoothly without too much interference, though it may go much better if a mother or teacher is in the offing to settle disputes, patch up quarrels, provide something new when play bogs down.

Any two Four-year-olds still express the tendency to exclude some unwanted third, but somewhat less than just earlier. Now friendships may be quite positive and based on shared activities and not merely on the exclusion of some unwanted other.

Cooperation, sharing, taking turns now tend to come quite easily to most. Interest may be directed more to the excitement of shared, cooperative activity than to attempts to control the actions of other children. In fact, the Four-year-old's love of big projects often makes the help of several other children necessary.

There is much less difficulty than earlier about owner-

ship of possessions as several can now play cooperatively
with the same material.

Children of this age enjoy the notion of "friend," and
a nursery school teacher can often stimulate a friendship
simply by announcing to a child, "Here is your friend
who wants to play with you."

Fours are not as rigid about interpersonal relations as

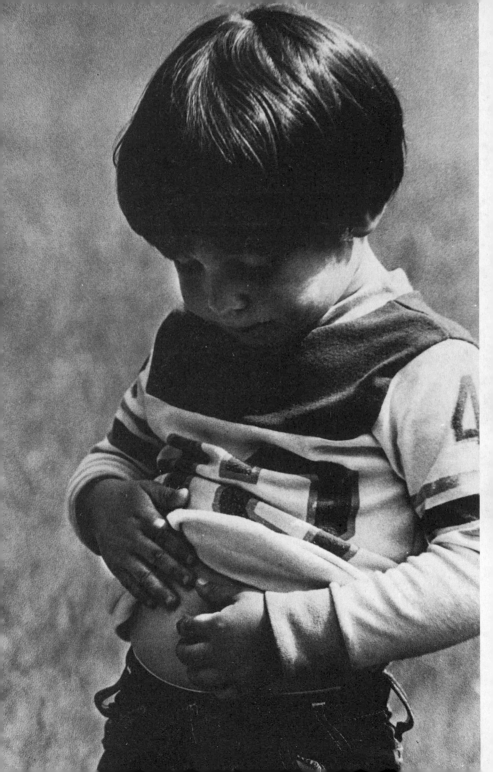

they were just earlier, so a mother or teacher can often solve any momentary tangle by humorous verbalization, by shifting the scene of play, or merely by suggesting some interesting elaboration of any current activity.

Or, the child himself may solve his own social problems: "First let me have a turn," or, "It's my turn now. OK?" Or, "Pretty soon will you let me use that red?" or, "Please, may I have my iron now?"

Four-year-olds, obviously, have all the words they need for any and all social relations: "Let's play with this. OK?," "I'm the dairy-farm man. Want some dairy cream? Who goin' help me get milk? Who goin' help me unload the barn?," "Put it on top. Yes, that's pretty good," "Feel my forehead. It's so hot," "My belly button's sticking out." Or, cuttingly, "Richard, you have big ears."

If, in a play group, several should sit at a table, crayoning or playing with clay, there is much interchild interchange. They may quarrel mildly over materials, show the teacher what they have made or what others have made. Or, while they work with their hands, they may discuss topics quite unrelated to what they are doing.

Four's typical violence and exaggeration express themselves in play with friends as in other activities. "I just set your coat on fire," a quite usual Four-year-old may say to his friend. When his friend ignores this bit of (untrue) information, he may repeat, "Can't you see? I set your coat on fire!"

(As a matter of fact, Fours tend to be obsessed by fire. A fire engine may be a favorite Four-year-old present. Or, the child wants a fireman's hat. And above all he may want to be a fireman when he grows up. But at the same time he might be deathly afraid of the fire alarm and need to be protected from his fear.)

Violent and excitable as he may often seem, the child of this age mostly wants his friends to like and approve of him. "OK?" is a frequently used expression: "I'll just take this one now. OK?," "Let's build a garage now. OK?"

In a group situation at this age there is very little isolated play. Children are now tremendously interested in each other as people, and they are also tremendously interested in, and ready for, group activity. Most children in any play group will spend most of their time in rather elaborate constructive or imaginative cooperative play. Frequently, now, children can organize a cooperative activity by themselves, without adult help or suggestion.

They may, as earlier, emphasize imagination. Or, they may emphasize actual construction and activity. One group may, spontaneously and without help, build a large block church and then conduct a service. They may build a store and then sell groceries. They may build a boat and then go for a sail. But their talk about any of these activities may be more important to them than the activity itself.

Friendships are strong at Four. Children not only like to play with their special friends but like to sit with arms around each other and whisper. Even boys can be seen hugging and kissing each other. If one of a pair of friends initiates an activity, such as painting, his friend will probably want to paint, too.

This warm interest in others can, and often does, lead to sex play if children are left unsupervised. Such play is probably not particularly harmful to children, but most parents don't like it. And obviously it can be overindulged in if not put in its right perspective. When it does occur, no one special child should be *blamed*, since any child, no matter how nice his mother may consider him, could be the one who starts it. Careful supervision can usually prevent such play.

But parents need to remember that tensional overflow often does have its outlet through the genital region at this time, especially in boys. Grabbing the penis in a socially tense situation is quite usual. This is no time to tell the child to "stop that." Better to direct the child's mind toward something of interest, such as going on an excursion through the house or yard.

In older Fours, especially in boys, certain children tend

to stand out as leaders. Others in a group quite willingly carry out their orders and do what they say. Girls tend to lead in a more romantic way. In a nursery school group, one or more of the boys may consider that they have fallen madly in love with some special girl, and these friendships may last for several weeks.

In a nursery group there tends to be strong identification with the group. Children will bring in food to share with everybody. They like to invite other children, as

well as teachers, to their homes to visit them. They love parties, and like to celebrate their birthdays, either at school or at home.

SIBLINGS

The Four-year-old can be an aggressive little fellow, with brothers and sisters as well as with those outside the family. Actually he may get on less well with siblings than with others. In a play group he tends to gravitate to those other children who appeal to him and whom he likes —his friends. At home he may be involved with children he has not selected and may not always like—his siblings.

A Four-year-old is usually old enough that unless he is having real emotional problems in growing up and in being superseded by somebody younger, he will much of the time be reasonably good to a baby sibling. But even now he should not be trusted alone with a baby, at least not for any long periods of time, as he is still not entirely predictable. (And if he is one who actively dislikes his baby sibling, they should not be left alone together for even a short time.)

With other siblings, Four is unpredictable. He may play nicely, but he may be extremely quarrelsome and rambunctious, even with those somewhat older than he. It is often surprising to parents that a Four-year-old can, on occasion, get into real trouble with a brother or sister considerably older. In fact, Fours can, for their own reasons, sometimes unfathomed, become extremely aggressive and directive toward much older siblings. Perhaps their own sense of superiority is threatened by greater competence. At any rate, a quite typical command, by a Four-year-old to an older sibling, may be: "Don't do it like that. That's wrong. If you do it again, I'll cut you in pieces and throw you in the garbage."

And though often good to those much younger, a Four-year-old may be surprisingly mean even to a baby, like the boy who, quite unprovoked, said to his little sister, all dressed up in a new pink dress, "Pink, pink, you stink." (Perhaps here he is exercising his sense of superiority.)

Households vary, and children differ. Some, especially quiet little girls, may get along with their brothers and sisters a good part of the time. Others are extremely quarrelsome and "always fighting." When such fighting occurs, parents should: 1) appreciate that fighting among siblings is not only normal but tends to be much enjoyed by them, no matter how much they scream; 2) separate them when possible; 3) figure out what times of day or what situations bring the most difficulty, and then, so far as possible, avoid or minimize those situations.

NURSERY SCHOOL

Though nursery school attendance is not essential for a happy childhood, one of the most satisfactory and exciting opportunities you can offer a Four-year-old is the opportunity of attending a lively, lovely, nonacademic nursery school.

Your normally endowed, characteristically exuberant, bursting-with-energy-and-with-a-desire-for-new-experiences Four-year-old may all too quickly exhaust your own most enthusiastic and generous efforts to keep him entertained. A good nursery school teacher has that second wind so necessary to keep up with the vigorous and demanding child of this age.

Equipment in a good nursery school can, quite naturally, be both more abundant and more varied than even a well-equipped household can be expected to provide.

Teachers, unlike mothers, are not looking after the child in the midst of other duties. Setting up a situation in which the child can fully express his own creative and dramatic interests is her job, her full-time job. And she is less likely to be called on to take part in his play than is his mother at home.

Not only is equipment more plentiful, adult help and guid-

ance more available in a good nursery school than in the ordinary home, but there are all the other children.

Other children at times excite but also at times calm down the sometimes too exuberant Four-year-old. There is perhaps no better learning situation for any child of this age than one in which he finds himself at the tender mercy of his contemporaries. Here, rather than from books or in forced learning situations, is where the child of this age *really* learns.

Few experiences can be more satisfactory for most preschoolers than a good nursery school. However, a good day care situation, especially if the staff members are well trained, nowadays offers for many Four-year-olds many of the same advantages. Though many working mothers wish they could stay at home with their child or children, day care may not only be necessary but can have much to offer.

chapter three
TECHNIQUES

The techniques with which one can best handle the bouncy Four-year-old stem directly from a knowledge of his basic personality. Obviously, the better you understand him, the better job you will do in helping him behave in ways that will please you rather than grieve you.

To begin with, Four is one who loves adventures. Share them with him. Create them for him. A simple trip around your own neighborhood, with its inevitable points of interest, takes on new luster when seen through the enthusiastic eyes of a Four-year-old. And when you plan an excursion, plan it with him in mind. A short walk, perhaps past a spot where a new building is going up (or, better still, being torn down), and an ice-cream cone on the way back will be a lot more satisfactory to a Four-year-old than a cultural expedition to a nearby town.

The best way to calm Four down when some of his wilder ways (his profanity, his boasting, his supersilly way of talking) bother you is to ignore him. "He only does it to annoy," as the old rhyme tells us. So, if you show that you not only are not annoyed but do not even notice, the thrill of profanity or exaggeration dies down, in most, rather quickly.

An opposite technique, and one that is more fun and perhaps equally effective, is to join in and enjoy. You will

25

not enjoy his profanity, but you can often enjoy his exaggerated stories by countering with your own—obvious—
exaggeration. That is, rein in when you feel that you
absolutely need to, but do not always rein in.

Certainly you can join in with and truly enjoy some of
the wonderfully silly poems and stories now available for
the Four-year-old. You haven't lived if you have never
shared with a Four-year-old the delightful nonsense of a
book such as Ruth Kraus's *I Want to Paint My Bathroom
Blue*, which tells you of

26

A doorknob a doorknob, a deer little doorknob.
A deerknob a deerknob, a door little deerknob.

Or, try some of the gorgeous rhymes in *Somebody Else's Nut Tree*, also by Ruth Kraus:

> There was a girl
> and she had a cat
> and a dog
> and a chicken
> and she wanted a horse.
> On her birthday
> she got a horse
> and that day the horse had horses.

Four loves his own familiar stories and songs, but, unlike the just-earlier child who must have everything just *so*, he may enjoy having a familiar story or song read or sung in a silly way. Thus, "Twinkle twinkle little star" might become "A bat and a rat sat on a hat." With each repetition, the song may be sillier and sillier. Many parents find that they are better at these games and exaggerations than they thought they were.

A very important thing for any parent of a Four-year-old is to try not to be aroused in a negative way by his often unacceptable behavior. If you appreciate that this kind of behavior is potentially there, you are less likely to be thrown by it.

If your child attacks you, as he sometimes will, with rude remarks, play a game of "insulting" to release his (or your own) pent-up feelings as though your name calling were real. Try such foolish epithets as, for instance, "You're a toasted marshmallow," "You're a squashed worm," until laughter takes over.

To be certain that you take the time for the excursions and adventures that the Four-year-old so loves, especially if you are very busy with his younger brother or sister, you may like to set aside one afternoon a week, or part of an afternoon, that will be *his*. He may choose (from a list prepared by you to be sure that things don't get *too* wild) the destination or activity that will please him for that particular week. He (or she) may even like to keep a little notebook, with considerable help from you, of course, that tells about these weekly excursions.

Since the child of this age does tend to go out-of-bounds, you will need, for safety, to find the most effective way of containing him within what you consider to be acceptable physical limits. Environmental restrictions such as gates or closed doors are not as effective as earlier, but most at this age do respond pretty well to verbal restrictions, such as "as far as the corner." In fact, the Four-year-old seems to like and respect boundaries and limits, which he doesn't have within himself. He seems to appreciate it when you supply them.

Most respond rather well to the statement, "It's the rule that . . . ," even when they do not understand why it is the rule. The statement "It's the rule" can, of course, apply to almost any situation throughout the day. It is wise, however, to use it only in fairly big and general situations, such as, "It's the rule that we don't hit other children," or, "It's the rule that we don't grab other people's toys." Don't waste this good technique or fritter it away on single situations, such as by saying, "It's the rule that you mustn't hit Johnny."

"It isn't fair" is another similar stricture that many will respond to even when they don't fully understand it.

Boundaries, or at least *shape*, can be provided if you give your Four-year-old a structure within which he can function. If, for example, he is visiting his grandmother, and his behavior becomes a little too wild, she can help him by telling him, "You are the *guest*." She can then outline a few restrictions that pertain to *guest*'s behavior, and it may be interesting enough to him to be a guest that he may to a large extent conform to reasonable restrictions.

With some boys and girls, a very good technique at this

age is bargaining. If it bothers you to do this, or if it seems too much like bribing, don't do it. But with Fours many parents find that a little bargaining goes a long way. That is, you give a little, and your child may be willing and able to give a little in return.

Since this is an age when children love "tricks" and new ways of doing things, sometimes, if a child balks or stalls, you can motivate him by suggesting that he hop or skip toward some desired destination.

Transitions do not present the difficulty they did some six months earlier, but if there is trouble with transitions this can often be countered by enthusiastic talk about the next proposed activity.

One general rule that may save you and your child much anguish is to try to avoid known trouble areas. There may be some things you do together, or some situations, that almost inevitably spell trouble. When you have identified such an area, do what you can to change the whole situation, instead of allowing it to arise and then disciplining on the spot.

One thing that from now on can make a great deal of difficulty is that most children *hate* it when their mother is on the telephone, especially when her conversations run on and on. They hate it; they behave badly and get into trouble and then make a fuss; and then their mother scolds and yells and punishes.

It is probably hard for a mother who may feel that she has little enough fun or time to herself during the day to appreciate how shut out a child feels when his mother is gossiping on the phone. It would be an act of great kindness, and would prevent much bad behavior and the accompanying need for punishment, if long, chatty phone calls could be restricted to some time when your child is having his nap or is otherwise out of the room.

A child of this age, since he so loves silliness, may respond better to some silly noun, adjective, or verb than to a more conventional instruction. If you tell him not

29

to push a friend, he may go right on pushing. If you tell him, "Don't be a goober [pusher]," he may respond more positively.

Although positive instructions tend to work better than negative—that is, tell him what you want him to do, not what you do *not* want him to do—the negative can at times be used effectively. An exaggeration of the negative, such as "Never, never, never!," if expressed forcefully, may engage his attention and his compliance.

It's best, in general, though, to keep things positive if you can. If you tell a child how nicely he is going to behave, he sometimes does so.

As just earlier, the child tends to respond very well to the notion of newness. Such words as "different," "surprise," "guess what" are still highly effective as motivators.

Or, some made-up word that has specific meaning only to the child and his mother, such as "cushalamacree," may at times be extremely useful. Such a word can roll off Four's tongue with ease and enjoyment. And when its meaning is secret, it can produce magic results, to the astonishment of those not in the know.

Thus one girl of Four always ran and hid when her mother came to fetch her from a friend's house. But just the saying of that special word, by her mother, helped her to organize at once, helped her gather up her things and walk out the door holding her mother's hand, feeling safe in the knowledge of this word that nobody else understood.

Whispering may, as just earlier, be more effective than shouting. At least it calms the child and catches his attention.

Distraction, at any preschool age, can be, as some have put it, a truly "magic wand." This technique will be less necessary with a fluid, fast, ever-changing Four-year-old than with the child just younger. But even at Four your boy or girl may sometimes get stuck on a point, and the two of you may find yourselves at loggerheads. If this occurs, rather than fight things through, you may be best advised to change the subject or the scene very quickly by any distracting device that may occur to you.

Since Fours love exaggeration, in your efforts to motivate or restrain, as well as in your efforts to entertain, you will find exaggeration to be very effective. "As big as the world," "in ten million years," or just plain silly language, such as "mitsy, bitsy, witsy," "goofy, woofy, spoofy," can often interest or distract when distraction is needed.

At Four, perhaps even more than at other ages, praise and compliments work wonders. Later on, children may be aware of exaggeration; but no compliment and no amount of compliments seem too much for Four's insatiable appetite. You can comment on a handsome shirt, a pretty dress, nice new shoes. Or, you can praise the way the child accomplishes any given task or any creative activity. Or, if he is playing with others, you can praise his relations with others: "I bet he appreciated the way you helped him with that."

In fact, if you don't praise enough, he will praise himself. You can often hear your Four-year-old expostulate, "I'm smart." You can smile and agree with him.

You can always win by telling the child how much you love him. It is easy and natural to criticize and to try to improve your child. If words of praise come less naturally, then they need to be cultivated.

Along this same line, remember that at this or any other age the simple act of conversing with your child can work wonders. Almost any child loves to feel that he has his parent's full attention, and he loves to talk. If you want to know what is on your child's mind, you don't necessarily need to ask directly. Just talk with him. Good communication is vital in those difficult teen years soon to come, but it is important even here. So, listen to your child and talk to him. Conversation provides one of the best routes to a good relationship, and in the final analysis *it is your relationship with your child even more than the use of good techniques that gets you smoothly through the day.*

There is one special aspect of the world today, often criticized and seldom praised, that can nevertheless help you out beautifully, especially on a rainy day. Do take advantage, freely though carefully, of one of the great new things society has to offer for the preschooler—television. All of a group of Four-year-olds recently studied by us did watch television.

All parents of boys and nearly all parents of girls felt strongly that TV did add to their children's lives—if only to their enjoyment. So, don't be afraid, within reason, to take advantage of what your television screen has to offer. It can be one of your best techniques for filling some of the day and for meeting Four's high demand for excitement, activity, and drama.

The choice of suitable programs may be difficult, especially if there are older siblings. So, try to select some one program that you consider good for your child that will become *his* program. Then he can be more easily controlled in not being exposed to other programs that may be both frightening and beyond his comprehension.

And if some program he watches attempts to teach letters and numbers or sizes and shapes, and he responds to this teaching, let his interest be your guide. It won't make him smarter, and it probably won't make him read any earlier than he otherwise would have. And it is just as well not to encourage him to show off any such skill to friends and neighbors. But if you and he enjoy this exercise, fine!

Last of all, remember that once you appreciate what a child of this age (or any age) *is* like, it helps you to appreciate what he *will* like. You can tailor your techniques accordingly.

DISCIPLINE

This discussion of techniques attempts to convey, at least implicitly, our attitude about discipline. Discipline, as most of you appreciate, is not the same thing as punishment. Discipline, rather, is a way of setting up the child's life situation so that good, effective, desirable behavior becomes possible. Techniques themselves are a form of discipline.

As to your own *philosophy* of discipline, you may be an old-fashioned, authoritarian parent who expects your child to do what you tell him to, regardless, even when the demand may be unreasonable or beyond his ability. You may be a *permissive* parent who permits anything and allows the child to follow his own whim.

Or you may, as we recommend, follow a policy of what we call *informed permissiveness* (or controlled flexibility). That is, you try to fit your demands and expectations to things that it is possible for a child with the maturity level and personality of your own to perform. Knowing that your demands are reasonable, you make them, firmly and consistently.

The more effectively you manage this, the better your discipline, the fewer will be the incidents of rebellion, disobedience, or "bad" behavior, and the less need for punishment. (Though no parent succeeds entirely. There will, in any family, be some unhappy incidents.)

As to what kind of punishment you should use, if and when punishment becomes necessary, this depends partly on your own temperament and partly on what works with your child. Temporary isolation works with some. Deprivation of privileges works with others. Some respond to scolding, some to more physical measures. An occasional spanking, if it works, is not immoral; but spanking should never be relied on as a chief form of punishment.

The so-called behavior-modification people hold that you can get any child to do anything you want him to by praising the good and ignoring the bad. This kind of handling seems complicated or unnatural to some, but for those of you who would like to try it, we suggest that you read *For Love of Children* by Roger W. McIntire.

Other disciplinarians have used (for some eighty years now), with reasonable success, a common sense kind of discipline called "logical consequences." That is, if the child does something he shouldn't do, or fails to do something he should, he must take the consequences. For example, he leaves his tricycle outside, and it gets stolen.

Each of you will, of course, work out your own philosophy of discipline and methods of discipline, keeping in mind both your own temperament and that of your child. Most important of all, perhaps, is that, if possible, Mother and Father agree, if not about every detail, at least about the basic approach. Two parents working together, especially if they have a reasonably good understanding of what it is reasonable to expect of their particular child, have a very good chance of helping him to behave in a comfortable and effective manner, at least much of the time.

THINGS TO AVOID

1. Don't worry excessively if your Four-year-old, as he very likely will, goes out-of-bounds. A certain extra exuberance is natural, usual, and quite probably necessary at this age to give balance between uncertain Three-and-a-half and quiet, adaptable Five.

2. Don't fuss too much and certainly don't worry if your boy or girl lies, swears, and/or exaggerates. Such behaviors are almost the essence of Four-year-oldness. You can, and undoubtedly will, discourage and disapprove of such behaviors, but try not to worry about them.

3. In fact, try to avoid excessive "moral" judgments about your child's often somewhat antisocial behavior. In another year he or she may be as conventional, as docile, as conforming as you please.

4. Avoid that wild search for things that will motivate an uninterested or underactive child. *Success* is the best motivator at any age. The likelihood is that any child will be motivated to activity if you provide for him materials and opportunities that by his temperament and matu-

rity level he will be able to cope with and to deal with effectively.

5. Don't worry that you should be doing something to increase your child's IQ. Basic intelligence level is, so far as we know, largely determined by genetic factors. You can and should give all children reasonable stimulation, but don't be self-conscious about level or quality of intelligence.

6. Don't feel that you should be teaching your Four-year-old to read. Read to him. Make books available. And when the time comes that he starts picking out initial letters in books or asking, "What does S T O P spell?," by all means respond. But don't push. Be sure that any interest in reading (or in numbers) that may be shown is his and not merely your own.

7. If your child is still sucking his thumb, fondling his blanket, or indulging in any other earlier tensional outlets, try not to feel that it is now "time" that he give these up. Another few months may see the behavior ended.

8. Don't feel that you have a "bed-wetting problem" if your child still wets the bed at night—some nights or even every night. Many quite normal children do not develop the ability to stay dry until they are Five or even Six, or even later. (Pad them up good and tight to save on laundry, and don't fuss or worry.)

9. Don't blame your child's playmates for behaviors in him or her that you don't like—exhibitionism, bad language, sex play, and the like. Today it may be a neighboring child who initiates the activity. Tomorrow it may be your own!

10. Don't fail to enjoy this extremely amusing, lively, enthusiastic age while it lasts, even though some aspects of your child's behavior may not be entirely charming.

chapter four
ACCOMPLISHMENTS AND ABILITIES

As long as your boy or girl is developing in what seems to you a reasonably normal way, if he behaves about as other children in your family have at his same age, or about the way other children in the neighborhood seem to do at his age, you should not be too self-conscious about specific abilities and inabilities.

It is important to remember that intelligence and maturity are two separate things. A child may obviously be very bright, but young for his age. Or, he may be not so bright, but mature for his age. And whether he is bright or not so bright, mature or immature, keep in mind two important things.

First of all, remember that intelligence is to a large extent an inherited capacity. You will, of course, want to give your child all the reasonable stimulation possible, make his life full and interesting. But even your best efforts will not, in all likelihood, make him more intelligent than nature intended. Even if he is not one of the more superior, intellectually, there can be a very good life ahead for him if you do not make his lack of A-quality intelligence a matter for major concern.

The same with maturity. Our expectations of what a Four-year-old should be able to accomplish are only averages, and a child might be quite a bit ahead of, or quite a bit behind, any time schedule that we or others set up, and still be perfectly normal. If your Four-year-old by chance does not seem quite up to usual Four-year-old maturity standards, this may mean that, when the time comes, you will want to have him go a bit more slowly in school than the law permits, but it still is not necessarily a cause for anxiety.

Any listing of the activities and accomplishments of the supposedly typical child of any age should be preceded with the clear warning that perhaps there actually *is* no truly "typical" child. When we describe Four-year-old behavior (or, for that matter, behavior typical of any age), we mean that most or many children of that age do behave that way.

But there will be many children who, because they follow the usual path of behavior change at a faster or slower rate than the average, will reach the behavior in question sooner or later than the average time. There will be many others who, because of their own individual personality, may actually never behave in quite that special way.

Consider an age characteristic such as the expansiveness and out-of-bounds behavior that we think of as so highly typical of the Four-year-old. If you have a gentle, quiet, moderate, restrained little boy or girl, he or she will in all likelihood be more expansive at this age than at Three or Five, but may not even at this lively age go to any great extremes. Or, if his or her whole rate of development may be a little on the slow side, even though intellectual endowment may be fully adequate, it could be on toward Five before the customary Four-year-old expansiveness appears. That is, the behavior in question may come in early or late.

As to specific abilities described in this chapter, here, too, you must allow your boy or girl considerable leeway. A child could be as much as a year ahead of, or behind, any supposed "average" and still be quite within normal limits.

For instance, interest in books and in formal learning varies tremendously. Or, a child may be ahead of age in some one behavior (language behavior, for instance) and not up to age in motor behavior. Each child has his own individual rate and pattern of growth.

MOTOR BEHAVIOR

Your typical Four-year-old, with his high drive, enthusiasm, expansiveness, is a motor person *par excellence*. He loves to run. He loves to climb. He loves to gallop. He loves sheer movement for its own sake. And, he loves to talk, to shout, to carry on. He loves exaggeration, of sound and movement as well as of actual words. He loves to talk about big (or enormous) things, and he loves to make big things. His drawing strokes are dashing, and he needs lots of room for his productions.

His drive seems boundless. There is strength and push behind everything he does, and he gives the impression of being ready for anything. A difficult motor situation, which may have brought out all his sensitivity and insecurity six months earlier, is now a welcome challenge. He loves the difficult and the daring. He loves the different. He loves to show that he is master of space and incline.

As we've said before Four is speedy. There is a quickness of decision and of action apparent in almost everything he does. He moves quickly and with very little wasted motion.

Four coordinates the movements of the parts of his body much better than formerly. In fact, he often shows a remarkably good ability to move his body effectively and to move it in relation to other things in the world. His increasingly good sense of balance allows him to play games requiring complex motor skills and to enjoy body-building skills and stunts. This may be a good time to introduce a few body exercises such as toe or knee touching, or making angels in the snow. The child appears

especially to take pleasure in stunts that stimulate the semicircular canals: whirling, swinging, somersaulting.

In fact, there seems to be an inner awareness of what he or she can do. More feelings seem to be unfolding now, combining the control of physical ability to move with the awareness of self and feelings inside one's body. This is why a child of this age enjoys creative movement, with perhaps the addition of drumbeat or song. (An inner awareness is also evident in his interest in stomach, heart,

and bones. His frequent reporting of stomachaches makes one aware of this concern.)

At times, his motor drive is so extreme that if he is *not* given opportunities for motor activity, for blowing off steam, he may become a difficult young person for those in charge to manage. If any Four-year-old is giving you trouble with his exuberant demand for action and variety, see to it that he spends as much time as possible out-of-doors, and hopefully that he is provided with plenty of physical equipment that will give him the opportunity to use and display his muscular effectiveness. He feels his muscles in activity, and he also wants *you* to feel his muscles and to tell him how strong he is. He may like to tell you, "I'm tough!"

Specific motor abilities of both balance and action have improved impressively in the past few months. The child not only walks upstairs a foot to a step but also walks down a foot to a step, at least on the last few steps. He can stand on one foot from four to eight seconds, can skip on one foot. He can accomplish either a running or a standing broad jump. He can jump down from a two-foot height with feet together. He can hop on his toes with both feet off the ground at the same time, seven or eight times in five seconds.

Many can learn to use roller skates. And some of the better coordinated can even ride a small bicycle if it is equipped with training wheels.

By Four, most children have acquired strength, ease, and facility in the use of their legs, which lend considerable grace to their movements. Most walk with long, swinging steps, in the adult style.

Boys, especially, and some girls, are rapidly becoming athletic, and take real pride in attempting motor stunts that require delicate balance. In ball play, most now use their hands more than their arms in catching a small ball. They can judge their direction of throwing better now than they did just earlier. Boys throw a ball overhand with a horizontal motion from above or to the right of their shoulder; girls from above the shoulder with a downward sweep.

Fingers are now much more skilled than earlier and under better control. Children can handle small objects, button or unbutton buttons, lace shoes, string even rather small beads. Most can cut on a line with scissors and can carry a cup of water without spilling. They enjoy games that involve many little pieces that need to be manipulated.

Though the Four-year-old is by nature active and athletic and loves to cover considerable space both on the level and in climbing, his increased attention span means that he can stay longer than he could before in a single area of activity. In fact, though he so greatly loves physical activity, he is able to sit for relatively long periods of time at an especially interesting manual task.

Hyperactivity. We hear a good deal nowadays about a way of behaving that has probably always been with us but that currently has a new name. When a child is overactive and seems never to stay still, can't quiet down, can't stick with one thing, can't turn his motor off even if he wants to, we label his behavior *hyperactivity*.

The truly hyperactive child finds it almost impossible to slow down and concentrate. As a preschooler he wears everybody out, and as he grows older he frequently finds it difficult or impossible to behave "properly" or to succeed in school because of his overactivity.

It is often difficult for parents of the active preschooler who is quite normally "always on the go," always "into everything," to distinguish between normal preschool activity and real hyperactivity. Your best bet is to check with your own doctor or child specialist.

VISUAL BEHAVIOR[1]

There is a fluidity, flexibility, and looseness in the visual patterns of the typical Four-year-old. He is definitely more stable visually than he was at Three, and definitely more outgoing in his visual response. His attention is to the horizon, and he often goes far afield in his pursuit of that horizon.

As his space world enlarges, he enjoys outdoor play, while indoors he prefers not to be confined to a single room or play area. In nursery school, his activities spill over from one room to the next, and even into hallways. Outgoing he is. Boundaries need to be carefully established lest he go too far and endanger himself, such as following a dog across the thin ice of a pond.

Four's high energy drive results in a new burst of physical activity. He is a charmer who has trouble telling the difference between fact and fable. He exaggerates as he practices using new and big words. He may roll his eyes in a delightful manner as he talks.

There is greater interest and participation, now, in both gross and fine visual-motor activities. Outside, he likes climbing equipment, ball play, a tricycle, and sometimes even a two-wheeler. The availability of plastic bats and balls makes a simple game of baseball even more fun. The newer, small-size two-wheel bikes make learning to ride without training wheels easier. If the youngster can touch the ground while the bike is upright, he will have less trouble learning.

The secret to balancing on a bike is through the hands, which tend to be in better control if the trunk is bent forward. Once a child can trust his hands, he'll be able to ride. Newer versions of the old-fashioned tricycle, with the sitting area closer to the ground, reduce the danger of

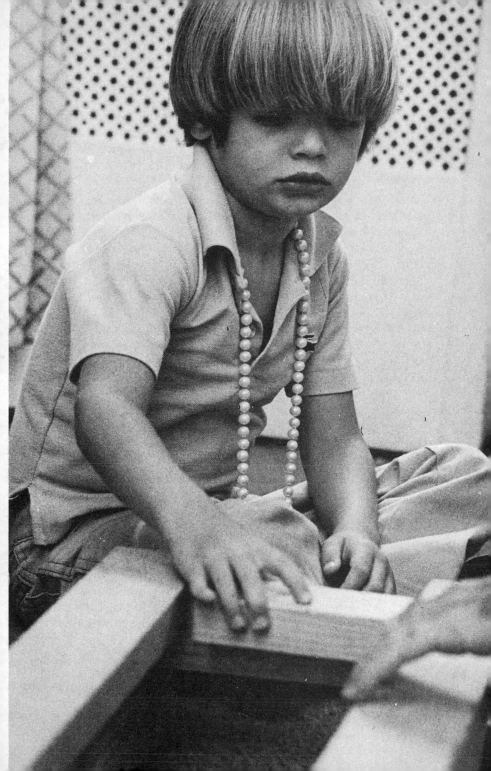

tipping. The heightened motor activity is not limited to boys alone. Girls enjoy it, too.

Drawing, coloring, and painting are becoming more successful for the Four-year-old than they were earlier. A good pair of blunt scissors is appreciated by the young craftsman or craftswoman. Puzzles, blocks, and other building materials are enjoyed.

Seeing is now action oriented. For this reason, the child may like to sit close to the television as if participating in the action on the screen. Parents should remember that television viewing is a poor substitute for activity at this action-oriented age.

Spatial language is well developed. The child can now react correctly to such prepositions as "on," "under," "in back of," "beside" or "in front of," when asked to place a ball in relation to a chair. And the child is now better than he was at following directions at home. He can find his own clothes. He understands about picking up toys and putting them away.

If there has not yet been a visual or eye examination, now is a good time to have it. Four can attend to directions, answer questions, and he is capable of concentrating for a period of fifteen to twenty minutes while such an examination is being made. When he has had enough, he may get down from the examining chair and leave the room. He escapes!

Good cooperation is possible if the examiner works quickly. The Four-year-old responds well to the simple E letter test, or he may know some of his letters, especially those in his name. Both of his eyes participate in the total act of seeing. There is better eye teaming and less need than earlier to support vision by bringing hands into the seeing act. There should be a normal amount of farsightedness measurable. His visual acuity may be close to 20/20 if not already there.

ADAPTIVE BEHAVIOR AND PLAY

Wild as your Four-year-old may be in motor ways, and even emotionally, when it comes to working with his hands you may be surprised to find a beautiful fining down. Eyes and hands coordinate with increasing skill, and fingers increase in their ability to make even rather fine and intricate adjustments.

Four can do many things that his Three-year-old self could not accomplish. Building with cubes becomes so increasingly skillful that he can now imitate a five-cube gate with delicately tipped center cube. By Four-and-a-half, he can make such a gate from a model, without watching it being built.

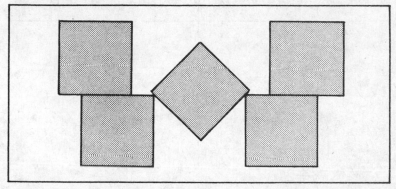

Figure 2

With pencil or crayon, too, he is becoming increasingly skillful. Whereas at Three he could imitate a cross, he can now *copy* a cross if you show him a drawing of one. And, at Four-and-a-half he can copy a square, a rather mature skill.

Or, he can copy the order of a group of things, such as stringing differently colored or differently shaped beads in the order provided in a model. Many can match all shapes, such as square, circle, star, etc., in a ten-hole formboard.

47

If asked to draw a person, the child can make a recognizable person, though it may still have a potato-shaped body and facial features may be included inside this body. Or, he may be able to draw a man with head and eyes, body, arms, and legs.

If asked to complete an Incomplete Man, most can now add five parts, including, usually, leg and foot, arm and hand, eyes or hair or ear. At Four-and-a-half, most add seven parts to the Incomplete Man—those seen at Four, plus, in many, a body line in the neck area—and their man often appears rather wild, with longish hair, longer arm and leg than six months earlier. Many now, with their characteristic special interest in bathrooms and belly buttons, add a belly button to their man. (*See* Figure 3.)

Four years   Four-and-a-half years

Figure 3
Typical Response to the Gesell Incomplete Man Test

Most children now really enjoy drawing things, and many enjoy coloring books, filling in the outlines reasonably well. Many adults feel that coloring books deaden the child's presumably innate artistic ability. We feel that they are not harmful if you are careful also to permit the child free artistic expression. Actually, many Fours especially enjoy tracing over the lines of the figure in a coloring book. They also enjoy drawings that provide dotted lines that when linked up make a picture.

The use of scissors is becoming rather effective. Many can cut on a line well enough to cut out pictures and then paste them onto paper or into a notebook in consecutive order. Or, they can cut a picture into parts and then put it back together again, puzzle-fashion. They also enjoy large and not too complicated picture puzzles, response to such puzzles becoming increasingly adept as they move on toward Five.

Adaptive behavior that also includes language expression may now have developed to the point that the child can give likenesses and differences between familiar objects. Or, he can tell the biggest and the longest of three things, and can order five blocks from the heaviest to the lightest, with few mistakes. He masters form both in matching and in placing.

Some Fours, especially older Fours, are becoming much interested in trying to print their letters and numbers. Some may even be able to print their whole first name, though usually in large, two-inch-high, capital letters. Though children should never be pushed into this kind of activity, when it occurs *spontaneously* it should be supported and encouraged, as should early efforts to read.

Play. Four's playtime is seldom a problem. He is ready for anything. Almost any kind of toy or material appeals, and whatever is lacking can often be made up for by his vivid, fertile imagination.

But he moves so rapidly, running through materials and situations and even space, that he may need a rather large quantity of whatever it is that he (or she) is using. Parents need to budget larger supplies of material, such as paper, at this age, but at the same time they need to determine limits of use. They will also find that it is better to set these limits prior to an activity than to clamp down when it is in full swing.

Fours may be happiest with rather active gross motor play, preferably out-of-doors. Most enjoy fully any opportunity for outdoor play. This does not have to be constructive or planned for. Almost any Four-year-old, with his exuberant energy, his vivid imagination, and his ability to turn almost anything into a good play opportunity, loves to be outside where space permits him the kind of activity he so much enjoys.

By Four, or certainly by Four-and-a-half, most can play outside in their own yard unsupervised, with only occasional checking by a parent.

One can readily see why the freer, more outdoor-oriented activities of the usual nursery school are better for the Four-and-a-half-year-old than the more structured and confined, indoor, kindergarten types of activities offered by some schools.

A Jungle Gym provides ideal equipment for the Four-year-old to climb on or on which to perform interesting tricks, such as hanging upside down or holding on with one hand. A slide for sliding, a good place to dig, a flat surface on which to ride his trusty tricycle will obviously add to his enjoyment, but even a relatively unequipped yard can be turned, by him, into a joyous place to play.

Hopefully, in summer there may be a short visit at the beach or in the country. Four is not too young to begin to appreciate the birds and trees and flowers—even though, unfortunately, many children in our cities are, and remain, far away from all the wonders of nature. Watch a Four-year-old hold a flower in his hand. Or a bug. He is full of awe and wonder.

In fact, for many, religious stirrings are there, and God may become a part of the child's vocabulary, his being, and his thinking. One Four-and-a-half-year-old boy, when asked what he liked best, summed up his feelings with "I love the sky and the mountains and the flowers and the whole world." The concept of wholeness now includes the

world, and Four may even think that the Fourth of July
is the whole world's birthday, not just that of the United
States.

Both boys and girls, but especially boys, relish almost
any vigorous physical activity, such as riding their tricycle
fast, sliding, digging. Building with big blocks is also a
favorite physical, as well as constructive, activity. Big
blocks are often combined into impressive structures—
houses, stories, forts. The child's big muscles seem to want
to lift heavy objects. Once such structures are built, children often play imaginative games inside. (Or, they love
any corner of a room, any secret place where they can
have privacy to giggle and whisper.)

Or, big blocks may be combined with trucks and wagons,
or cars and trains. Boys, especially, may construct elab-

orate roads and tunnels or tracks, one or two leaders often bossing a "gang" of workers. Whether they combine them with block structures or not, boys love cars and trucks and trains and airplanes—anything with wheels.

Fours, also, in their search for adventure and for anything new, very much appreciate excursions, exploring trips, visits to museums, or even simple walks in their own neighborhoods.

Four's vivid imagination often leads to dramatic play of the most creative sort. No kind of "pretend" is beyond him. Within half an hour, children in a group may be monsters, astronauts, robbers, storekeepers. Or, the child may pretend he is a photographer taking somebody's picture with a Polaroid camera, waiting a minute, and then showing the imaginary result.

Of course, inevitably, they play house, little girls usually taking the part of mothers, grandmothers, and babies; boys of fathers, grandfathers, or people coming to sell something. (Or, if no better role is available, that of the family dog.) Playing store is almost as popular as playing house, with everyone wanting to be the salesperson behind the counter.

Or, less imaginatively, children love to "help" wash cars, wash floors, wash windows. In fact, almost any sort of water play is extremely popular. Parents tend not to be too friendly toward this. They are afraid that their children will spill the water or get themselves wet. With a little effort and ingenuity, most could make more readily available this interesting, satisfying, and soothing kind of play. Blowing bubbles is especially delightful to Four and can as a rule be quite easily controlled.

Doll play, the most conventional form of imaginary play, is becoming increasingly elaborate. Dolls go to a picnic, go to nursery school, or even move to another city.

Dressing up is very big at Four. Boys as well as girls love to dress up, preferably in adult clothes. Boys, as a rule, prefer cowboy hats and holsters; girls love long gowns, veils, hats, handbags. Boys are less likely than earlier to dress up in high-heeled shoes or women's hats. Make-believe weddings, with the bride, especially, dressed elaborately from the old-clothes box, are popular.

All the usual creative activities are still great favorites: crayoning, painting, fingerpainting, cutting, pasting. Some are starting to make letters and numbers spontaneously. Play-Doh and clay are still much used by younger Fours, but as children move on toward Five this kind of play may seem too tame for them.

Many other forms of earlier play are still enjoyed. Children like to build with plastic blocks or tiles or Lego or Tinkertoys or small wooden blocks. Most Fours like dominos or puzzles or simple card games. As they move on toward Five, they may begin to like games where points are scored, though it will require a mother or teacher to tell them how many points they have earned. Also, winning and being first are very important.

Books are still great favorites with most and make up a big part of the lives of many Four-year-olds. Whether being read to or "reading" for oneself, many now have special favorites and can stay a long time with a single book. This is the age when humor in stories is especially appreciated. Nearly all love such silly books as *I Want to Paint My Bathroom Blue*, *Somebody Else's Nut Tree*, or Stoo Hemple's *Silly Book*.

By Four, tastes in reading, aside from the general love of the ridiculous, are often rather individual and well defined. Some like whimsical or imaginative stories like *Curious George*, *Mulberry Street*, or *McGillicut's Pool*. Others prefer books about "real" things.

Since Four is an "out-of-bounds" age, it is not too surprising to find that the Four-year-old has a voracious appetite for the dramatic, and that no storied situation seems fantastic enough to overtax his constantly inventive imagination. Thus, complexity of event and even horror of situation seem to add value to many of the Four-year-old's favorite stories. Executioners and miraculous rescues from destruction have much the same appeal that the

Grimms' fairy tales afford. However, caution must be exercised to protect the vulnerable child who cannot tolerate a fear- or tension-provoking story.

Children of this age like complexity in illustrations. They enjoy an abundance and diversity of tiny details. Whereas the Two-year-old preferred a single large picture to a page, the Four-year-old delights in searching out minutiae in illustrations to stimulate and satisfy his constantly expanding interest and imagination.

Music is now a source of great enjoyment for many— not only the somewhat passive pleasure of listening to

favorite records but, especially in groups, more active participation. Older Fours can beat out a rhythm rather well and may like to "conduct" group singing with a conductor's stick. They also like circle games that combine singing and skipping around.

Television, as mentioned earlier, is becoming of increasing interest. Nearly all Four-year-olds do watch television except in those rare instances where there is no set in the household. Girls, usually more amenable, as a rule accept their parents' ideas of what and when to watch. Boys, too, usually accept parents' decisions as how long they should watch, though they may on occasion object to their parents' choice of programs for them.

Most parents do admit that, though it may create some problems, television viewing does add to the young child's life since it keeps him quiet and entertained. Many do feel that it must be limited or it becomes too engrossing. Some object because they feel that it is a passive activity. Others complain that it gives a distorted view of life. Most adults, however, do appreciate the relief it gives them, even while they may complain.

Pets provide a good deal of pleasure and experience about life for Fours as for children of other ages. There is much to be learned from pets, and if not too much is expected from him the young child can learn a great deal not only about living and growing but also about responsibility from the care of simple and relatively undemanding pets. But if the parent will not take the major responsibility, it may be best not to have a pet.

Short-time pets—snakes, frogs, caterpillars that can be contained in a terrarium—can offer much interest and excitement and may need not too much care. And turtles are all-time favorites. They may even develop a personality for the child and are often much loved.

Even less demanding is the care of sturdy plants, which still require a certain amount of responsibility. Even a Four-year-old can identify strongly and can enjoy the fact that his plant is surviving and growing partly because of the care he may be giving it.

LANGUAGE AND OTHERS

The Four-year-old tends to be an egocentric little person, but his egocentricity, perhaps happily, includes his contemporaries. Any Four-year-old who may be playing in a group that includes other children and one or two adults directs nearly all his conversation to the other children and is also reasonably responsive to conversation directed to him by the other children. Though he may from time to time speak to an adult, or acknowledge something the adult may say, his chief and outstanding interest tends to be in other boys and girls.

At this outgoing age, there is relatively little solitary play, and even when there is, it is accompanied by very little verbalization. Even when a child is not talking to others, what he says tends to have a social implication, as when a boy comes into a playroom and remarks, "Oh boy! What a noise!" Or, mimicking an adult's admonition, he may remark, "If I don't stop that noise!" Four is a noisy age—the Four-year-old is loud and active in most things he does.

Children by no means ignore an adult who is present or playing with them. It is merely that they are much more interested in other children than in adults. Thus, a child may give what he considers interesting information to the adult: "I don't mind anything. Anything 'cept when Mommy washes my hair," "I live next door to a haunted house."

He may tell or boast of his own abilities: "I can write," "I can count," "I can swing by my knees," "I'm awful strong," "Watch me jump. Awful high." And he boasts about possessions, comparing them favorably to any that others may have: "I have bigger blocks at home," "I got more blocks than the other children have."

He still is not above asking the adult for help: "How do you do this, anyway?," "Will you put this somewhere it won't get lost?" He may still, for all his improved social skills, sometimes ask for help *against* other children: "They won't let me have my car," "They won't let me come in."

If no other children are present or available, he may carry on elaborate imaginative play with an adult. Thus, a boy may initiate an elaborate game of telephone repairman, telling the adult what he is going to do and then carrying it out elaborately, with appropriate verbalization.

But his chief conversation now is definitely with other children. As at Three, he is most interested in conversation he initiates himself, though he is now highly responsive to things that other children say to him. And, conversation now reflects a much more secure sense of self. The child no longer seems to need to protect his every product or possession.

So, there is less talk about ownership, more asking permission to use things that others are playing with, more use of the word "let's," more friendly suggestions in cooperative play: "Could I have those tickets?," "First let me have a turn?," "Let's play with this," "Shut dat door. You see, we don't want any germs to come in," "May I please have the iron?" ("Please" is a favorite word for many at this age.)

Imaginative play tends to involve delightful verbal fantasy: "I'm the farmer. Who's going to help me unload this hay?," "I'm off to work. You put the baby to bed."

Or, cooperative play may involve the use of real objects, especially constructive materials, and practical conversation: "Put a roof on that house, why don't you?," "Ready?," "That's pretty good, but we need another one," "I'm holding it so you can get down." In cooperative play, Fours are quick to accept suggestions from each other. Any one incident of cooperative and/or imaginative play may continue for as much as twenty minutes, with good, sustained reciprocal conversation throughout.

As six months earlier, some children still seem to define those they like by emphasizing those they do *not* like, so excluding and rebuffing remarks are still very strong: "You can't come in," "Get outta here." Or, when one child, in imaginative play, remarks, "I need some more milk," another may retort, "That's not milk. That's only blocks."

They exclude children they don't like but often verbalize strong expressions of friendship for those they *do* like (of either sex): "You're my playmate," "I'm sitting with you," "I like you." They may show jealousy of a friend: "Barbara, don't you talk to him."

Fours love whispering and secrets. They now seem to have fun with language. They enjoy rhymes, and most adore silly language: "My mother's gone goo-goo," "Ready weady, steady weady."

The Four-year-old is, above all, a boaster: "I'm bigger than you are," "I can jump higher than you can." He boasts about his parents, or quotes them as ultimate authorities: "My mother says you can't have that truck." (Sometimes this boasting gets him into trouble with Five- and Six-year-olds. A fight may be the only way out, and the poor Four-year-old usually ends up in tears.)

Silly language is so loved by many that it provides an excellent technique for getting cooperation. Four seems captivated by any silly approach. And, language of any kind is extremely important now. In fact, in some episodes of imaginative or cooperative play, there may be more talking than action.

VARIANT BEHAVIOR

Inevitably at stormy Four, some violent physical resistance and even an occasional tantrum may be expected when things go wrong. For the most part, though, when he does not wish to comply or conform, the child's objections can be expressed quite effectively in his colorful language. He tells you in words, rather than in actions, why he doesn't want to do as you wish.

The child of Four, in a standard behavior examination situation,[2] which permits a fair comparison from child to child and from age to age, as just earlier, refuses with words and not with deeds. As Figure 4 shows clearly, at Four the child refuses things that do not interest him or look too difficult, in very close to what will also be his Five-year-old manner. Quite maturely, he neither fights nor cries. He just talks.

LANGUAGE AND THOUGHT

The child of Four loves language. He loves to talk, to rhyme, to whisper, to sing. Or even to shout. He is his

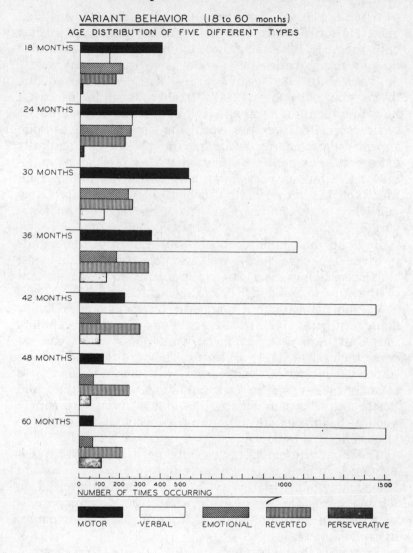

VARIANT BEHAVIOR (18 to 60 months)
AGE DISTRIBUTION OF FIVE DIFFERENT TYPES

18 MONTHS

24 MONTHS

30 MONTHS

36 MONTHS

42 MONTHS

48 MONTHS

60 MONTHS

0 100 200 300 400 500   1000   1500
NUMBER OF TIMES OCCURRING

MOTOR   VERBAL   EMOTIONAL   REVERTED   PERSEVERATIVE

Figure 4
*Age Distribution of Different Kinds of Variant Behavior,
from Eighteen months to Five years*

own self-appointed commentator and often his own audience. He loves words, likes to try them out, likes to play with them. He likes new and different words. He likes to do silly things with words, such as to say "smarty-warty" or "batty-watty" or "ooshy-wooshy." He even likes to talk to his play objects, especially if they don't do just what he wants them to: "You silly red ball," "You foolish block."

He especially loves the word "big," a word that is soon superseded by "enormous" or "gigantic." Four just naturally exaggerates, as we have mentioned: "as high as a mountain," "five million years," "as long as the world." In fact, much of his prevarication, which his parents probably call lying, may at times result from his tendency to exaggerate.

By Four, most children begin to use most of the sounds in their language fairly well. Some estimate that most English-speaking American children use about 90 percent of the American English vowels at this time.

Vocabulary has now increased by leaps and bounds. Some estimate that an average Four-year-old vocabulary may contain as many as 1,550 words. Most Fours can express themselves freely and well. They are now even more interested in stories than earlier, will look on when read to, may even ask what certain letters spell. If the child has been a television watcher, he may even be surprisingly good at saying letters and numbers, though it should be of no concern if he cannot.

The Four-year-old doesn't really *need* to know his letters and numbers, though as children move on toward Five, many quite naturally become much interested in written words and in knowing what certain combinations of letters spell. In fact, many can print their own names in capital letters.

Sentence structure, grammatical usage, and correctness of tenses is improving. As Laurie and Joseph Braga[3] point out, "Children do not learn to speak by copying adults. They listen to adults, learn the rules, and then make up their own sentences based on the rules they have at the

62

time. Children seem to have a built-in language-learning device that lets them learn to use certain rules about their language from what they hear. They even make mistakes in a systematic way."

For example, when they begin learning the rules for making plurals, children who previously had used the correct plural forms for "mouse" and "foot," now, at Four, say "mouses" and "foots." This is called overgeneralization, and is a sign of growth, a sign that they are learning the rules. Later they will learn the exceptions to the rules— again through listening, not through lessons, and will again say "mice" and "feet."

Somewhere around Four, most begin to learn the following word-changing rules: 1) When using "she" or "he," there is an *s* added to verbs in the present tense. Thus, "She walks," "He runs." 2) An *-ed* added to the verb means the past tense. Thus, "Today I walk to school; yesterday I walked to school." 3) An *s* added to a noun indicates more than one: "one dog; two dogs." 4) When something belongs to somebody, you use words like "my/ mine," "your/yours," "his/hers," "their/theirs."

Irregular verbs come in due time. But Four goes by his own simpler rules; thus, he "builded a house" and "knowded" he was right, before he takes on the irregular verb forms of "built" or "knew." He also adds extra *s*'s for possession, as "This is hers house."

All these things come in in their own good time, and some children, especially boys, are slower than others. Enjoy these transition forms as a part of growth, and be concerned only if the child doesn't move on to the usual forms by Five or Six. *It is important not to correct your child's language.* Fear of failing can make a child anxious and might even lead to stuttering or not saying anything. If they make a mistake, you can answer them, or repeat what they have said, correctly, but don't emphasize their own mistakes.

Between Four and Five, most learn to say some of the more difficult speech sounds such as *l, r, s, t, sh, ch,* and *j.*

And what they say is now largely intelligible even to those outside the family.

This is a top age for questions. Endless "whys" and "hows" are uttered, partly in pursuit of knowledge, partly just for the fun of keeping a conversation going, and partly in resistance, such as "Why?" meaning "Why do I have to?" However, the word is used most as a request for information: "Why does the wind blow?," "Why does the sun shine?," "Why does it rain?"

Since children of this age tend to be insatiably curious and avidly seeking for information, try to answer these "whys" as long as you feel that real curiosity and interest motivate them. Don't hesitate to cut short their conversation when they use their "whys" for stalling or resisting.

Not only does the child ask the adult for information, but he, too, likes to *give* information. He has a great deal to say, to adults as well as to other children. He likes to tell outsiders about things at home, and he especially likes to talk about his mother: "My mommy has a brand-new washing machine." He likes to provide facts: "Dogs can run very fast," "A pencil is a simple thing."

Or, he makes extremely touching personal remarks, like the little boy who said to his teacher, "You know, I often think of you. You could come to my house some time, and we could play ball."

Words aplenty he now has under his command. Conversation now truly enriches his life and his relationship with others.

By Four, most children can even define a few words by telling how they are used. Thus, they can tell you that an apple is to eat, a coat is to wear. Most also know prepositions, such as "off," "in," "next to" or "beside," and "on." They can also repeat after you a short sentence, say their numbers from one to ten, count three pennies with correct pointing. They can also carry out somewhat complex commands. A "test" that most Four-year-olds can pass is the instruction to "Close the door, put the book on the chair, bring me the key," or some variation of this kind of command.

Also, the child of Four usually has enough understanding of the relationship of parts to wholes to be able to tell you when something is missing from an ordinary object, such as an arm from a coat, or a leg from a table or chair. Or, he can tell you what everyday objects are made of, such as a chair is made of wood or a window of glass. Somewhere between Four and Five, on the average, comes the ability to name correctly the four basic colors, though actually some children are able to do this much earlier. Color naming seems to be a highly individual matter.

Most Fours can also respond correctly to such questions as "What cries?," "What swims?," "What sleeps?," "What bites?" And they can also answer correctly one of two such questions as "What must you do when you have lost something?" or "What must you do before you cross the street?" Language has come a long way for most.

chapter five
THE FOUR-YEAR-OLD
BIRTHDAY PARTY

Four is perhaps the first age when the very characteristics of the age lend themselves ideally to party giving and party going.

The average Two-year-old is not really certain what a party is. Is it the cake? The ice cream? The guests?

Three enjoys a party more or less as he would a morning at nursery school or an afternoon of play with a friend. He is on the verge of awareness that a party is something special and exciting, but often only on the verge.

Four, however, can be an ideal party age. The Four-year-old tends to be a creature of boundless energy, enthusiasm, and appetite for the new and different and exciting. He *loves* an occasion!

Though Four's enthusiasm can sometimes go out-of-bounds, he can be truly cooperative if things are exciting enough and are going his way. He tends to be extremely appreciative of adult attention. He throws himself fully and positively into plans for his own entertainment.

It is easy to entertain a party-giving or a party-going Four-year-old if you yourself have time, energy, goodwill, and imagination. He tends to accept quite uncritically the games you suggest, the food you serve, the favors and surprises you provide. (Five may say, "Oh, I have one of those." Thirteen may mutter, "Oh! One of those!" Not so with the Four-year-old.) Four's demand for something special or something new and different is easily satisfied by simple favors or attractive decoration.

Discipline should not yet be a major problem, at least for the mother who understands children of this age. She knows that a party is not the place for lessons in sharing, behaving, minding. Quarrels should be settled as quickly and inconspicuously as possible by removing one of the quarrelers or by providing some different but acceptable toy for one of two grabbers.

KEYS TO SUCCESS

The keys to a successful party at this age are speed, simplicity, and novelty. Speed is necessary because Fours react quickly and they tire rapidly if the party drags or if it lasts too long. Simplicity is important because children of this age are not mature enough to understand or to participate in complex games. Some novel element is important because Fours, unlike Threes, have a general notion of what a "party" is and expect something to go on other than just to go and play. This surprise should be something quite simple, such as a distribution of favors.

Number of Guests. Six guests is a good number and definitely not more than eight (both boys and girls). It may be safe to invite one or two extras, or at least to have some in mind who can be invited at the last minute. There are apt to be casualties among invited guests, so that they do not get to the party. They may be ill from overexcitement, their mother may not be able to get a baby-sitter and so cannot bring them, or other difficulties may get in the way.

Number of Adults. The host or hostess's mother and one adult helper need to be available. One or two of the mothers may need to stay as at Three—that is, mothers of children who are extremely shy or extremely aggressive, or who for other reasons may need to be there.

SCHEDULE

One and a half hours is plenty, ideally from 3:30 to 5:00. This timing allows for a nap beforehand for those who still need one, yet doesn't bring the refreshments too near dinnertime.

3:30–4:10   Guests arrive and play with toys. Parents bring, or earlier may have brought over, something for each child to play with (in addition to what the home may provide) for this initial period. So, the living room somewhat resembles a nursery school playroom, with a good assortment of toys, including big cars and trains, a rocking horse, dolls and carriages, stuffed animals, Blockcraft, Tinkertoys, big musical tops. Children play, usually quite individually, with these toys. The host or hostess opens presents as they come.

4:10–4:15   As children go into the room where refreshments are waiting, each one is given a favor. Fireman's hats and badges make good favors. These may be available on a table, and are given to each child as he or she goes into the dining room.

4:15–4:40   Refreshments have all been set up in advance on card tables or on low children's tables. (Tables may have to be borrowed.) Use a paper tablecloth, napkins, plates, and bright cups. And provide some kind of favors—for instance, little toy frying pans filled with candy. Balloons—all blown up—hang in a cluster on the wall. These are given to the children toward the end of the party.

The refreshments can consist of simple small sandwiches, the smaller the better, but in interesting shapes. Better for children to eat several small sandwiches apiece than to half-eat one big one. Or, sandwiches can be omitted and you can have just ice cream, cake, and milk. Individual frosted cupcakes may be better for eating, but there should be a central cake with four candles on it, which can be blown out.

4:40–5:00   Informal play period. Children play with the toys in the living room and with balloons, which have been distributed. (If balloon play becomes vigorous, it may be necessary to push toys to the edge of the room to allow space.)

If the children are on the older side of Four, some slightly organized play, such as singing games, play with instruments, marching, or dressing up in costumes, could be introduced at this time. Also, this is a good time for giving out special surprise favors. These are wrapped separately and may be presented in a big cloth bag that the children reach into, taking turns. They unwrap and play with these. Good favors include small figures of animals or humans, small balls with elastic, toy wristwatches, toy rings, fire trucks.

5:00   Departure. Mothers who are already there leave with their children. Other mothers call for their children. However, by the end of the party most Fours are tired and excitable and may cry or go to pieces if they have to wait to be called for. Thus, it may have been arranged for the mothers already there to take all the children home.

HINTS AND WARNINGS

Remember that you can count on only minimal group activity. Individual informal play is better than organized games for most. In fact, it is not only unnecessary but may be dangerous to introduce even simple games. Ring-Around-the-Rosy or Farmer-in-the-Dell would be better than some-

thing complex, such as Pin-the-Tail-on-the-Donkey, if games must be played.

Every child is likely to think that it is *his* birthday, wish it were his birthday, or pretend that it is his. So, all may want to blow out the candles. If someone other than the host or hostess gets there first, you will simply have to relight the candles.

There are almost bound to be some tears, some spilling, some disagreements or quarreling. Be especially careful that the party does not last too long. Fours tire easily and become overexcited.

As to favors and gifts: If you have hats, sturdy home-made ones are better than purchased ones, which are apt to rip and tear. Blowers may become a menace as children blow them into each others' faces. Don't have favors, sur-prises, hats, etc., all at the refreshment table. It makes for too much confusion. Have the surprises spread out a bit through the party instead of giving them all at once.

71

chapter six
HELP WITH ROUTINES

EATING

By Four, most children can feed themselves completely except for cutting. They are competent enough now at feeding themselves that they don't have to think so much about it or try so hard. Most can talk and eat at the same time now, though, in some, talking may definitely inter-fere with eating.

If the child's incessant talking interferes with adult enjoyment of the meal, some families still find it works best for the child to eat apart from the family. If he does eat with others, he tends to become restless long before the meal is over, and may need to interrupt his meal to go to the bathroom.

If parents are relatively relaxed about what the child eats, and unless a feeding problem has been built up in the past by poor management, there should not be much fuss about *what* is eaten. But many parents still worry about *how much* is eaten and may insist too much on quantity.

It is important to remember that the Four-year-old appetite may still be only fair, even though as the child moves on toward Five appetite may increase. Refusals and preferences are not quite as definite as earlier, but the child may still go on either food jags (insisting on the same thing over and over) or on food strikes (certain foods or types of food being definitely refused).

By Four-and-a-half, most can pour milk from a pitcher without spilling, and most drink their milk rapidly and well.

Those who eat alone are apt to dawdle, but they do not need to be fed, merely encouraged to speed up a little. Sometimes such incentives as eating to get big, racing with the baby, finishing within a certain time, or working toward a dessert goal may help. However, in general, the less gimmicky things become, and the less emphasis is put on the whole thing, the better. If children think that their eating matters a good deal to their mother, they are likely to use the power this seems to give them. A very casual attitude on the part of the adult usually works best.

By Four-and-a-half, children not only feed themselves nicely, but may even help to set the table. Both speed and appetite pick up. The child can usually manage more meals with the family, and is beginning to find a reasonable balance between talking and eating.

Though it is not within the scope of this book to discuss in any detail matters of either diet or health, and we do not wish to make any parent overly anxious about the kind of food eaten, we would like to give one warning. This is that some of the foods your child may like best may conceivably be harmful to him.

Obviously, if they make him sick to his stomach, or make him break out in a rash, you will know it and will avoid such foods. But as physicians concerned about child behavior[4] are now pointing out, many foods harmful to the individual child may do no observable physical harm but may have a disastrous effect on his *behavior*.

Food or drink, or even things that are inhaled, may produce hidden allergies, which, in turn, can cause extremely deviant behavior. In some children, dizziness, listlessness, fatigue, irritability, violence, and hyperactivity all can be induced by foods liked best.

Doctors report many striking examples of this, like that

of the boy who at Five had for two years been wetting his pants several times a day as well as having to get up several times during the night. This urinary difficulty, as well as other symptoms of overactivity, cleared up when he stopped eating tomatoes. Unfortunately, in this case, as so often, the boy craved the very food that was harmful to him. For two years he had had tomato soup for lunch every day, and would eat five or six ripe tomatoes at a sitting. His symptoms returned when (as an experiment) he was given tomatoes again, and cleared up when they were once again removed from his diet.

Or, even without there being an actual allergic reaction, harmful food products, especially artificial colorings and flavorings, have been shown to produce dizziness, listlessness, fatigue, irritability, violence, and hyperactivity, and, in school-age children, problems usually described as learning disabilities.

If your child seems healthy and happy, and if his behavior is reasonably satisfactory to you and to him, that is, if he or she is getting along all right in major ways, chances are you don't need to worry about all this. But if behavior is disappointing or unsatisfactory in major ways, and you can't find the reason, at least consider the possibility that something in your child's diet may be at the root of his difficulties.

SLEEPING

Bedtime is now relatively uncomplicated in most. In fact, some seem to know when they are tired and may even ask to go to bed. As at earlier ages, the child will enjoy some special attention, as a story read by his mother or bedtime singing. He may also enjoy half an hour alone in bed with books or crayoning, and often takes dolls or toy animals to bed with him.

The highlight for many a Four is that he is old enough to have earned the right to sleep in a big bed. Parents often produce their own bedtime problems by moving the child from crib to big bed too soon, as early as Two-and-a-half, especially if a new baby has come along. It would have been better to have two cribs, one for each.

Parents can often utilize this momentous experience of having a big bed at Four for potential transitions into release of younger behaviors. The crib shaker and head banger may even be cured overnight. The bed wetter may suddenly become dry. And the lovely, cozy expanse of a big bed may encourage a happy going-to-bed time, with room for a parent to lie down, too, as bedtime stories are read or prayers are said.

Bedtime is usually around 7:00 or 7:30 though with daylight saving time it may be later. If the child can read the time on the clock, and some can, he may respond better to the fact that the clock says it's time to go to bed than if Mother tells him.

A few children need to have not only a going-to-bed time but also a putting-out-the-light time. Without this extra few minutes to settle down in their beds with the light on, they may be very demanding.

Most sleep well, waking only, if need be, to go to the toilet. Some can manage this by themselves; others need substantial help from a parent. And still others resist being wakened and therefore should not be disturbed. This is not a big age for nightmares, though especially around Four-and-a-half some do have troubling dreams.

Many sleep eleven hours or even longer, waking around 7:00 A.M. The child is now able to put on his bathrobe and slippers if they have been laid out for him, can close the window, go to the bathroom, and then will usually play in his room until it is time to go into his parents' room. (Very young children may stay in bed not at all after they wake up. By Three, they *may* stay in bed until you tell them they may get up. By Four, many will wait until a certain hour [the clock says such-and-such] before getting out of bed.)

Though a few still really nap at this age, most have only play naps or no nap at all. Boys are more likely to go to sleep at naptime than are girls. Even if they do not sleep, here as just earlier even a play nap gives both parent and child a welcome change of pace, and a rest from each other.

The day's schedule, at Four, is often helped by the fact that many Four-year-olds enjoy the idea of a routine or schedule. They seem to like to know what comes next and to be able to count on it.

ELIMINATION

By Four years of age, things go pretty well with most. Most children are dry during the day and can manage this entire routine themselves, "Accidents," if any, tend to occur simply because the child does not want to interrupt his play and puts off going to the toilet until too late. If this happens repeatedly, a mother had best take some responsibility here. She can either see that the child comes in to go to the toilet at fairly regular intervals, or, if he resists this idea, she can tell him that she is going to blow a whistle when she thinks it is time for him to come in.

Many demand extreme privacy for their own bathroom functions now but show much curiosity about the activities of others. They are also very curious about strange bathrooms and may insist on seeing the bathroom, if visiting.

Out at play, especially if play is unsupervised, boys may like to urinate in front of other children, and there may be much silly talk about this function.

Perhaps the majority by now can stay dry all night if picked up around midnight. But it is not unusual for a child still to be wet at night. This, as a rule, should cause no concern. And if the midnight pickup does not ensure a dry night, it may be best to skip it altogether. Just pad the child up good and tight to save on laundry, and make very little comment about this immaturity.

(In fact, many quite normally developing boys and girls are Six years old or even older before it is easy for them to stay dry at night. So, it may be helpful for you to know that there are now available effective and reasonably inexpensive conditioning devices that in many instances can serve to dry up a child in a matter of weeks.)

Bowel movements in most are also usually rather well routinized, and this function, too, causes no problem in most. One movement a day, after either breakfast or lunch, is a common Four-year-old pattern, though some have more or fewer than one a day, or their functioning may occur irregularly.

As with urinating, most consider this an extremely private functioning and usually want the bathroom door to be closed or even locked.

Unfortunately, there are a few boys who are not up to standard in this department. There are some troublesome children, usually boys, who though they may be trained for dryness, seem to be making no progress whatever with regard to bowel functioning even as late as Four. They refuse to use the potty chair or toilet, and continue to defecate in their pants.

This refusal and continued immaturity of behavior tends to be related to severe mother-child battles. This is one way the boy who *must* control his mother finds it possible to do so. Most mothers will interrupt almost anything they arc doing if they feel that by doing so they can keep their son clean.

Some mothers have found that one way to solve the problem is to require the boy to wash out his own underpants. In some, this cleans up matters in a very short time.

Perhaps a kinder approach is one that we have long recommended. After checking with your pediatrician to rule out any physical reason for this delay, we suggest permitting the child to play in the bathroom, with his pants off, at about the time of day when you expect him to function. (If his functioning has not yet settled down to any particular time of day, you will just have to admit that you still have a long way to go.)

Put a newspaper on the floor in a corner of the room,

and tell the child that when he is ready he may use the paper. Often he is able to get this far in just a few days— a few weeks at most. Once he has succeeded with this, it is often just a small step to get him to use a potty— best in saddle potty form or a potty chair. From there to the adult-size toilet is usually fairly easy.

BATH AND DRESSING

The bath is now an easy routine, the child often being capable of washing himself fairly well as long as his mother suggests part by part what should be washed. Otherwise he is apt to get marooned on some one part of his body and wash that over and over.

Most can now let the water out of the tub and can wash out the tub (after a fashion). And can dry themselves (after a fashion). Most can also make the necessary wrist-and-hand motions to do a reasonably good job of brushing their teeth, combing their hair, and washing and drying their hands and face. Many can now wash their faces without soaking shirt or blouse.

Time of bath may now be shifted to before supper, if the family schedule permits, since the child is less tired at this time and can do a better job of washing himself. And oh, how he loves to play in the tub with all his bathroom toys!

The child of this age often dresses and undresses himself without too much help, though clothes may need to be laid out for him, each garment correctly oriented, since a few may still have trouble distinguishing front from back. If any special garment gives trouble and makes the child angry, you can plan ahead for the future as to just how he can manage that particular garment more successfully. (Or, ask yourself, Why is the garment so difficult? Is it really appropriate or necessary?)

Special difficulty may occur in relation to buttoning, though most now unbutton with ease. Fortunately, with modern zippers, less buttoning is demanded than formerly.

At Three-and-a-half, a good many children give much trouble about getting dressed. They resist and object. Four, as a rule, likes to dress himself, is proud of his increasing abilities, and may like to beat the clock or otherwise race to complete the process.

The majority can distinguish front from back, button some buttons, get shoes on the right feet and even lace them. (Some children consistently put their shoes on the wrong feet, and why this does not produce discomfort is hard to say.) Some can tie a knot in their shoestring but cannot yet manage a bow. Many boys, as well as girls, now *love* to dress up in adult clothes—hats, shoes, belts, scarves, skirts, pocketbooks—at playtime.

TENSIONAL OUTLETS

The Four-year-old seems much less tense than he was just earlier, at Three-and-a-half. There is less facial twitching, less stuttering, less blinking. There is even somewhat less thumb sucking, though many do still suck their thumbs, especially on going to sleep. Some have now given up their security blanket, though they likely still cling to their favorite stuffed toy. Some have replaced thumb sucking with nail biting and/or masturbating. Any of these behaviors may be expressed not only in private but even in public, as in nursery school at story time.

If tension is felt, it is more likely to be expressed in a large, gross-motor way, the child running, kicking, shouting. Tension may be experienced more in the genital region than in the facial region. Boys, in times of anxiety or excitement, may clutch their genitals.

Both boys and girls in social situations or at other times of excitement or strain are apt to have to go to the bathroom. This need is real and should, of course, be respected. Some may actually have toilet accidents in a demanding social situation if they do not get to the bathroom in time. A few may feel tension pains in their stomachs and may on occasion actually be sick to their stomachs with excitement.

However, when a Four-year-old feels tense and keyed up he may simply express this feeling in general overactivity, in running around and shouting or in talking too fast or behaving too wildly, rather than in the smaller and more specific ways (as thumb sucking or blanket fondling or nose or eye twitching) of just earlier.

Health in most is reasonably good, though a few seem to have one cold after another all winter. At this age, if the child falls down (as he often does) he tends to fall on his face and may very possibly knock out a front tooth. (At later ages he seems more likely to break his collarbone or his arm when he falls.)

chapter seven
YOUR CHILD'S MIND, OR DON'T PUSH YOUR PRESCHOOLER

For all the talk we hear nowadays about the cognitive development, or the cognitive training, of preschoolers, it is most important that you not be self-conscious about all this. Without your doing very much about it, you will find that the normally endowed Four-year-old is a creature of tremendous curiosity, wild imagination, delightful creativity. You will want to answer his many "whys" and to encourage his imagination and creativity. But don't take too seriously the sometimes-proposed notion that it is all up to you to teach him to think.

Especially, *do not feel that you must teach your preschooler to read.* Hopefully you will read to him, and read to him some more. Hopefully he himself may enjoy looking at books. And if by chance he is somewhat advanced and is already asking what certain letters mean, or is trying to spell out words, give him the help and encouragement he seeks.

But do not push. It really doesn't make a bit of difference in the long run whether he begins reading at Three or Four or Five or Six or even Seven. If your child should show spontaneous interest in letters and numbers at an early age, fine for him but no special credit to him or to you. If, on his own, or through the stimulation of certain television programs, he should, fairly early, come to recite

the alphabet or to say some numbers, so be it. Let him enjoy this activity, but don't take it as a sign that he is ready for early entrance to kindergarten.

In fact, try not to worry too much about your child's so-called cognitive development. It is almost, of recent years, as if psychologists and educators had discovered the child's mind. They rather give the impression that one must *teach* the child to think, and that it is necessary to provide all sorts of techniques and materials by means of which his mind will develop. It just isn't so!

So, try not to feel that you as a parent "ought" to be

doing something special about your child's intellectual life. Dr. Arnold Gesell commented long ago, "Mind manifests itself." The child's mind is not something separate from the rest of him. It manifests itself in almost everything he does, except perhaps through such purely reflex actions as swallowing or breathing. It manifests itself when he runs and jumps and climbs, when he shouts and laughs and sings, when he plays with his real friends or with his purely imaginary companions. A child who paints a picture or throws a ball is giving expression of his mind in action.

In fact, virtually everything the young child does is an example of his mind in action. It is not necessary for him to learn letters and numbers before he goes to kindergarten to show you, and others, that his mind is in good working order. If your boy or girl has good potential, and if you provide a reasonably rich and lively environment and give your love and attention, the mind should take care of itself.

Whatever his age, you do not have to be specially concerned about teaching your preschooler to think. If you provide a usual environment that contains a reasonable number of friendly, interested, sharing people, a reasonable number of books and toys and creative materials, a usual number of games and jaunts and pleasant excursions—the usual attributes of comfortable family living—he will learn as naturally as he grows and breathes. *Let us all relax!*

And here let us give you a specially important warning. Young Four-year-olds will, in the normal course of development, very shortly be turning Five, and you will be thinking about school for them. They will very soon be taking that important step of starting kindergarten.

And here is where all too many parents make that fatal mistake, which, for many children, stands in the way of school success and more or less guarantees failure, or at least academic difficulty, in all the years to come. They start their child too soon.

Regardless of what the law may permit in your particular state, we prefer to start children in school, and to promote them subsequently, on the basis of their behavior age rather than their age in years or their intellectual level.

It is the age at which a child is behaving, not his birthday age, that should ideally determine the time of school entrance. Thus, your child might be Six years of age come September and might have a decidedly high intelligence quotient, but if in his behavior (which can be determined by simple behavior tests[5]) he is only at a Five-year-old level, he will be best suited in kindergarten, with others who are behaving at this same level, rather than in first grade.

If your own school system does not offer prekindergarten screening and you have no way of finding out about your own particular child's behavior level, then you will more or less have to go by his chronological age.

In that case, we urge all parents to be very sure that that boy or girl is on the older side before he starts school. And since boys, as a rule, develop more slowly than girls, it would be best if your daughter is fully Five years of age before she starts kindergarten in September. Your son will do best if he is fully Five-and-a-half.

Teachers and administrators from all over the country tell us that it is the "fall babies"—children who have their fifth birthday in the fall after they begin kindergarten—who have the most trouble. They often have trouble not only in kindergarten but in all the years to come.

So, though we do not think that the notion of developing or improving your child's mind should be a matter of great concern for you, many parents are understandably interested in the way any child's thinking develops.

Here, then, are a few clues as to the ways that in general children's concepts of time, space, and number do develop in the usual child; a few clues as to the level of thinking often attained by the Four-year-old in such basic areas as sense of time, sense of space, sense of number, and sense

of humor. Here, also, is information as to what one may expect in the way of creativity in the child of Four.

SENSE OF TIME

Four may still seem young compared to what comes after, but the ordinary Four-year-old is actually a rather sophisticated person when it comes to his sense of time.

The child of this age seems almost equally at home, verbally, in past, present, and future, and use of tenses is usually accurate. Such a common time word as "day" is used in many different inflections: "today," "this day," "every day," "another day," "once a day," "day after today."

Generalizations include such somewhat sophisticated words and phrases as "for a month," "once a day," "usually."

"Time" is included in many compound words: "lunchtime," "dinnertime," "every time," "sometimes," "one time," "almost time," "meantime," "for a long time," "Our time is over," "Is it time?" Even such broad generalizations as "springtime," "summertime," "wintertime" are now used quite glibly.

Or the seasons can correctly be put in their context: "next summer," "last summer," "this winter" are used correctly.

And so far as "minute" goes, not only can the child say, and mean, "in a minute," but also "in five minutes," "this minute," "a minute ago," "just a few more minutes."

"Week" and "month," too, are used effectively, such as in "next week," "some other week," "next month," "for a month," "in a month." "Night" and "morning" are comfortably used in many expressions, such as "late at night," "early in the morning."

Children are beginning to grasp the sense of seasons and activities related to seasons.

Most seem to have a reasonably good understanding of when events of the day occur in relation to each other.

Four-year-olds can, as a rule, tell not only what we do

at Christmas and Easter but also what we do at Halloween, though Thanksgiving is still beyond most. Most Four-year-olds still cannot tell correctly what time they go to bed, have supper, get up, go to school.

Though most girls can tell their age correctly by Three-and-a-half, most boys are Four before they can give this response correctly, most often by showing four fingers. Four-year-olds cannot, as a rule, tell when their birthday comes.

SENSE OF SPACE

The space world of the Four-year-old, like so many aspects of his living, is definitely expanding. Outstanding at this age is the use of expansive space words characteristic of the out-of-bounds, expansive tendencies of the Four-year-old. Some of these words have been used before, but are especially noteworthy as a group at this age. Typ-

ical are "on top of," "far away," "out in," "down to," "way up," "way up there," "way far," "out," "way off," "way out," "out in."

"In," "on," "up in," "at," and "down" are space words perhaps most often used. As the child climbs on his Jungle Gym he is experiencing all these changes in space, and this may be why a Jungle Gym is such a favorite with Four-year-olds.

A new dimension is suggested in the frequent use of the word "behind." The Four-year-old tends to be much concerned with the backs of things. He wants a book to have a back as well as a front. And if his book has a house on the front cover, he anticipates that the back of the house will be on the back of the book.

He is especially interested in his own back and hopes he can view it with special mirrors. As two Four-year-olds, enamored of David Brinkley on television, watched him but saw only his front, one of them was heard to say,

"My daddy says David Brinkley has a back, just the way we do."

And, finally, most Fours can now tell both on what street they live and in what city they live. They can put put a ball *on*, *under*, *in front of*, and *in back of a chair*.

SENSE OF NUMBER

The ordinary Four-year-old can count, with correct pointing, three objects. Many are reported to count to ten, though they may start their counting with a number higher than one. Verbal counting, that is, rote counting, without objects, definitely exceeds counting of objects.

Stimulated by television, some children nowadays can count by rote even higher than ten, but this does not in most instances constitute any real understanding of numbers or an ability to count real objects.

Their hands provide at least ten units. Let them use their fingers as they wish. This is the way children learn naturally.

And, Fours love double numbers like 44 or 66 or 77. They also love games that include numbers, as beanbag throwing.

SENSE OF HUMOR

The typical Four-year-old is gloriously humorous. From a loud guffaw to a subtle, sly wink, he runs the gamut of humorous expression.

Nobody will ever appreciate your own humor more— so enjoy yourself while this full appreciation lasts. Enjoy the child's humor and enjoy his enjoyment of your own!

Four loves silly language. He loves the ridiculous. He loves the imaginative. He loves the very fact that *you* have a sense of humor and are making a joke, even when he may not fully understand what the joke is about.

He especially appreciates it when *you* appreciate *him*. Silly or funny books are among the things he appreciates most, and are among the things that you can enjoy together.

Four is not above the same kind of humorous appreciation one sees at Two and Three—anything that goes wrong: a shoe on the wrong foot, a sweater sleeve that sticks, a hat on backwards.

But he now has moved, also, into the somewhat subtler realms of humor. In his own spontaneous storytelling he demonstrates the kinds of things that seem funny to him. Thus, a Four-year-old child, in his stories, may think very funny something like:

A car went the wrong way. It broke the ceiling. He ate up her door and her whole house. He ate up hisself. He ate the whole world.

I had a silly dream about a talking tractor.

The mother clowns came. They made funny faces. Boy found anudder monkey and then the monkey did laugh.

By Four-and-a-half, most humor has not proceeded too much farther in the direction of subtlety. In typical stories, children of this age tell us:

David's mother pulled off my mother's nose. And then my mother pulled off David's mother's nose.

Rabbit, he ran. He got caught in a trap. He couldn't get out of the trap. Ha! Ha!

The girl shook when she took a look. And the tree shook. The whole world shook. A head shook.

The great thing about Four is that he can on occasion be really quite funny from the adult point of view, and even when he isn't, he so enjoys his own humor and is so ready and willing to share his enjoyment and his joke that his attempts at humor are amusing for you as well as for him.

CREATIVITY: SPONTANEOUS STORIES

The ordinary Four-year-old is a great one with language. He loves words—loves to hear them and loves to utter them. Rather surprisingly, then, it may be more difficult for you to get him to tell you a story than it was just a few months earlier. Now he may feel self-conscious about what a story is. Whereas when younger, with fewer words at his command, he might blithely proceed to "tell a story," now he may feel that this requirement is too hard for him.

A little persuasion usually suffices. And once embarked on a story, Four is fluent, glib, and often surprisingly violent. Three-quarters of both boys and girls express some kind of violence in their stories—accident, aggression, harm to objects or people. Falling down seems to be the leading type of violence for girls—boys stress things breaking or broken.

Not only do many bad things happen in Four-year-old stories, but for boys, at least, Four is the low point in the entire preschool range for kind or friendly themes.

Here, as earlier, there is a rather marked difference between the sexes in feelings expressed about parents. Though boys at this age see their mothers as entirely friendly (caring for, providing, sympathizing, protecting), girls seem to see their mothers as primarily disapproving, disciplining, punishing, or hurting them. They see their fathers as friendly. Boys in our group do not mention their father in stories.

Another clear-cut sex difference is that girls talk mostly about mothers or girls in their stories; boys talk about boys.

People who worry about the effect of violence on TV on preschoolers might be surprised to know that small children in their spontaneous storytelling (and this was true long before we even had TV) often rival or outdo the largest amount of violence one may see on the screen.

Girls at Four are more violent in their storytelling than at any other age, earlier or later. Their stories now stress death, killing, things eaten up, objects that crash or fall down or are burned up, children throwing things into the garbage or being spanked or broken to pieces.

Fantasy predominates, and stories have now moved from the home or immediate community and many are laid in unfamiliar or distant places. A typical girl story:

A little ducky. He fell in the water and he drowned. His mother came along and she picked up her ducky and threw her in the garbage pail. Then a frog came along and swallowed her up. And then the frog was so big he ate up everything. You know what else he ate? He ate the whole world all at once. You know what else he did? He ate up her door and her whole house. And the next morning you know what else he ate? He ate hisself.

Don't grab anything from toys when children have them. Balloons you blow up and sometimes they break. If the ants eat your house and break the stones and make holes in the stairs 'cause they want to live there you can't get into the house. If you eat food and throw the dishes they break and you get spanked. You throw them and cut yourself and you get spanked. You get a needle and punch it right down your arm and then you bleed. If you throw books you get spanked by some-body you don't know.

Boys, too, emphasize themes of violence. Things in their stories are burned up, broken, fall into the water. People are killed, go to the hospital, are kicked, fall, are eaten up, hurt, crash, or die. As with girls, stories are laid primarily in somewhat distant or unfamiliar places, and fantasy predominates over reality. A typical Four-year-old boy story:

Boy got killed from a rocket. And then another boy came and he got killed from the rocket and then another boy came and he got killed. And then another boy came and that missile killed him. And then another boy and the snowman came and a girl came. A snowman got on the rocket and went scuffing around and flying away. . . . The car broke. The motor crashed. It crashed into a truck.

CREATIVITY: IN GENERAL

Though some children are by nature much more creative than others, there is a very great deal you can do to encourage creativity in your enthusiastic, outgoing, spontaneous, though sometimes combustible Four-year-old.

Even by Two or Three years of age in some, and quite certainly by Four, you may have determined whether your own particular child is by nature primarily a hearer, a talker, a toucher, a mover; whether he or she is most affected by sounds, colors, words.

Some best show their creativity by combining words, some by combining shapes and colors, some by combining ideas, and some through their own physical movements.

Lise Liepmann, in her own highly creative book— *Your Child's Sensory World*, suggests the following creative opportunities that you might like to provide for these different kinds of children.

The child who primarily experiences through hearing may enjoy listening to music and (later on) creating his own musical sounds. Or, he will enjoy listening to books and stories and then telling his own stories, dictating to a tape recorder, or playing any and all word games.

The primarily visual child may be the one who most enjoys crayoning and painting, and working with paper— especially colored paper—and paste and scissors. And if he has good fine-motor coordination as well, he will enjoy stringing beads in creative design, in making (very simple) models, or playing with Tinkertoys or Lego blocks.

If your child is a toucher, right from the beginning clay and fingerpaint may be his favorite materials. And if he is a mover, dancing, running around, climbing, swinging, sliding, or simple acrobatics—each of which can include its own creative aspects—may provide his favorite forms of self-expression. Or, he may prefer fine-motor to gross-motor activities and may combine imagination with the movements of his hands in finger play or puppets.

These are, of course, just a few of the many things any preschooler may enjoy, and any child may very likely find pleasure in a combination of many different kinds of interests.

It is generally agreed, both by child specialists and by artists themselves, that children are best encouraged in their creativity if you permit much freedom of enterprise. Adults will do best by enjoying and permitting the child's own enjoyment of art works that are less than "perfect" and that do not necessarily resemble what the child set out to make.

Efforts to have them copy from models, and criticisms of less than perfect products, tend to stifle the child's own spontaneous creativity. That he work in any medium with enthusiasm and enjoyment is obviously more important than that he produce some special product.

The young child creates primarily to please himself, but he also likes to please those around him. Admiration and praise can hardly be applied too lavishly when the child is only Four. He loves the things he makes, and he loves to have you praise them.

We sometimes think of creativity in relation chiefly to paint and painting, but as Milton A. Young points out in his imaginative book *Buttons Are to Push*, the young child can create not only with almost any conceivable material or equipment, but he can create without any material or equipment other than his own often vivid imagination. Some children show perhaps their greatest creativity in their spontaneous play with their imaginary companions—human or animal—or in their own impersonation of an animal.

If you want to give your child what we *usually* think of as a good opportunity to develop his creativity, you will provide crayons and paper, fingerpaints and paper, or waterpaints and paper. By Four years of age, some of the products he will make with these will be pleasing to him and may even seem attractive to you, his parents. Modeling clay, too, provides a customary and gratifying medium for creative and artistic expression. Puppets please many.

But there are many other things you can do to encour-

age creativity in your preschooler. Here are some of the special activities that Young and others recommend. Most of you will also have your own favorites.

Go for a walk and talk about the things you see.

Suggest that your child look for shapes in the clouds.

Watch birds together and try to identify them. Build bird feeders, birdhouses.

Make a (simple) treasure map and then have the child follow the map to find a treasure.

Play hunting games with "hot" and "cold" for clues as to whether the child is getting nearer to or farther from the object sought.

Help your child keep a notebook. It could be a notebook of birds, of flowers, of cars. Or, it could be a notebook about the trips and excursions you take together. He could cut out and paste in pictures himself. The text or titles, he could dictate to you.

Ask your child to draw a picture of an animal that does not live on this planet, and to explain how it lives.

Or, put several common household objects in a bag and tell the child to feel them (without looking at them) and to identify each one. Then ask him to make up a story, including each one.

Play simple word games, asking your child to name all the things that can fly, all the things that are red or green or blue, things that rhyme with certain words.

Ask him to describe something without looking at it.

Ask him to be very quiet and then listen to the sounds he hears and tell you about them.

Start a two-line poem and ask the child to think of a final word to rhyme with the last word of the first line.

Present your child with a simple problem situation— what would he do if such-and-such a (simple) crisis should arise.

Actually you don't have to ask a Four-year-old to tell you a story, or even play word games or set up such specially stimulating situations as listed above. If you have an imaginative child (and most Fours seem to be highly imaginative) and have even an ounce of imagination yourself, just a plain conversation with a child of this age can be fun for you both. Four is so appreciative that he quite inspires an even halfway imaginative adult. Few people will ever be so appreciative as he of your slightest whimsy.

If he's telling you about all the magic things the Black Knight can do, ask him if he knows about the Green Knight. He'll be delighted if you tell him that the wicked Green Knight steals a little boy's shoes and his parents think that *he* has lost them.

Or, he will tell you, if indoctrinated by a religious grandparent, that if the Devil punches *him*, he will kill the Devil with his shining sword. He will listen with interest while you explain that, so far as you know, the Devil harms children not by punching them but by *tempting* them. A discussion of temptation can be long and fruitful.

You don't need toys or even books, you need only words—yours and his—to have a more than satisfactory playtime with a typically lively and imaginative Four-year-old. Each family may have its own special imaginative games. After swimming, one boy we knew liked to lie down on the sand, all covered up with towels, pretending he was a cocoon. When you touched the cocoon gently, you could see a butterfly emerging. It began by his lifting one arm and leg under the towel, stopped if you approached too quickly, and closed up again. This activity repeated itself until finally a beautiful butterfly was there in all its glory. (But you had to watch out, for it could turn into a poisonous insect if it chose. Anything can happen, with a Four-year old!)

Or, finally, though some may not go along with the idea, you could watch selected television programs together and then talk about *them*.

Whatever you choose, try not to formalize any of these creative activities. Keep the situation fluid and be very careful about your timing. When the child's interest fades, it's clearly time to stop.

chapter eight
INDIVIDUALITY

We have been describing ways the Four-year-old may be expected to behave. But this does not mean for a minute that all Four-year-olds will actually behave in these ways. *Every child is an individual and different from every other child*, even from others of his own age, sex, or background.

There are many different ways of looking at personality and of describing individual differences—some systematic, some hit-or-miss. Though in this chapter we shall lean mostly on the systematic classifications of constitutional psychology as offered by Dr. William H. Sheldon, in his book *Varieties of Temperament*, we would like to remind you of some of these special differences we mentioned in our earlier book on *Your Three-Year-Old*.

Some of you might like to check on your own boy or girl to see if he or she is one who could be described as having high drive and high energy, or low drive and limited energy. You could check to see if he is one who might be described as highly focal, tending to concentrate on a single activity, or, if of a more peripheral nature, he finds it hard to concentrate and settle down.

Is he a perseverator—one who goes on and on with some single activity—or is he one who tires easily of any one task or situation and flits quickly on to something else?

Is your child one who organizes from within, or is he

chiefly influenced by people and things around him? Is he one who starts himself, or do you have to wind him up and start him?

Is he one who is mostly influenced and controlled by his intellect, or does he work mostly through emotions? That is, can you appeal to him intellectually, or do you merely work on his feelings?

Is your son or daughter one who adapts very easily to the environment, or does the environment have to do the adapting?

Is he speedy or slow? Is she messy or spotless? Does he look forward or backward, do best if you warn in advance or if you spring things at the very last moment?

Is he a perfectionist, never satisfied unless everything is perfect? Or is he casual and careless, quite satisfied with a lick and a promise and then on to something else?

These are but a few of the dimensions of difference that you might like to identify, and then respect. You yourself can probably think of many other pairs of characteristics and then identify your own boy or girl as being like one or the other of the pair.

A more systematic approach to the fascinating area of individual or personality differences is that offered by Dr. Sheldon. His system of constitutional psychology proposes that behavior is a function of structure and that we can to quite an extent predict how any child will behave from an observation of what his body is like. Though no individual is *all* one thing or another, there are three main components that go to make up the human constitution, and in most people one or the other does predominate.

These three components are endomorphy, mesomorphy, and ectomorphy. The body of the endomorph is round and soft; that of the mesomorph hard and square; that of the ectomorph linear, fragile, and delicate.

In the *endomorph*, arms and legs are relatively short as compared with the trunk, with the upper part of the arm longer than the lower part. Hands and feet are small and plump. Fingers are short and tapering. In the *mesomorph*, extremities are large and massive, with upper arm and leg equal to lower arm and leg in length. Hands and wrists are large, fingers squarish. In the *ectomorph*, arms and legs are long compared with the body, the lower arm longer than the upper arm. Hands and feet are slender and fragile, with pointed fingertips.

Recognizing your own child's body type and knowing

how endomorphs or mesomorphs or ectomorphs customarily behave, or are thought to behave, may help you fit your own expectations closer to reality than might otherwise be the case. It is sometimes easier to understand and accept your child's behavior if you believe that he behaves as he does because of the way his body is built rather than if you think that sometimes less than ideal behavior is either your fault or his.

According to Sheldon, then, the endomorphic individual is one who attends and exercises *in order to eat*. Eating is his primary pleasure. The mesomorph attends and eats *in order to exercise*. What he likes best is athletic activity and competitive action. The ectomorph, on the other hand, exercises (as little as possible), and eats (with indifference) *in order to attend*. Watching, listening, thinking about things, and being aware are his most enjoyable activities.

Another clue to the differences among these three types is that when in trouble the endomorph seeks people, the mesomorph seeks activity, the ectomorph withdraws and prefers to be by himself.

Time orientation, too, is something that may vary with physical structure. Our experience has been that the endomorph tends to be most interested in the here-and-now. The mesomorph seems to be forward looking. The next thing or the new thing is what interests him. The ectomorph seems interested in past as well as future.

It may help you to identify and to know what to expect of your own boy or girl if we tell you something about the way children of each of these three kinds of personality behave in ordinary life situations. Even in things as basic as eating and sleeping and relating to others, we see big differences.

EATING

The typical *endomorph* loves food. He may almost be said to live to eat, and he will eat almost anything. Even when not eating, he likes to be doing something with his mouth like chewing gum, sucking a lollipop, or enjoying a nice soft drink. Mealtime is seldom a problem with such a child, except that he may tend to eat too much, too often.

The *mesomorphic* boy or girl is less enthusiastic about food but still tends to have a big appetite. If you do not, by your insistence on certain specially disliked foods, spoil things, the mesomorph, as a rule, does not give too much difficulty in the food department. He consumes large quantities of food and usually eats rapidly.

Not so with the *ectomorph*. Mealtimes for him may be the hardest time of day. Appetite tends to be very, very small, and even the mere sight of a plate heaped with food may turn off what little appetite he has. Color and texture of food may also turn him off. He may refuse to eat anything mushy, or lumpy, or of the wrong color, as, for instance, "Those little green balls [peas]."

The ectomorph can live and thrive on much less food than most parents think he needs; and five small snack-meals a day might suit him better than the customary three large ones. Don't push, and he will as a rule comfortably decide on his own nutritional needs.

SLEEPING

The *endomorph* not only loves to eat but as a rule he also loves to sleep. He snuggles down contentedly with his thumb or teddy bear, and enjoys nap or night sleep, lying limp and sprawled in almost any position.

The *mesomorph*, as a rule, is also a good sleeper. He drops off to sleep quickly and easily, sleeps soundly though often with much thrashing around. He often seems to need less sleep than do other children, and is one who wakes quickly and easily, jumps out of bed and then wakens you, cheerfully, at 6:00 A.M. or even earlier.

The *ectomorph* has trouble with sleeping, as with eating. He finds it hard to get to sleep but once asleep finds it hard in the morning to wake up and get going. He needs a great deal of sleep, but it is hard for him to fall asleep unless he is close to physical exhaustion. He sleeps lightly and dreams a great deal. That is, his relaxation, even in deepest sleep, is incomplete.

REACTION TO OTHER PEOPLE

The *endomorph* likes people, and people like him. He is warm and friendly with others, and they tend to feel relaxed and comfortable when they are with him. He does not, even as a young child, like to be alone.

The *mesomorph* likes people, too, but he is nowhere near as dependent on their company as is the endomorph. However, he usually has plenty of friends and is a natural-born leader, even in his preschool years. As a rule, other people have to adapt to *him*. He gets on best as a leader or as the one the others look up to. He likes others primarily because of the things they can do, because of the activities they can enjoy together.

The *ectomorph*, in contrast to the other two, has a strong need for privacy. He likes to be alone and dislikes to be socially involved. If he has a choice—which the young child does not always have—the ectomorph avoids being too much involved with other people. He tends to be distressed, uncomfortable, anxious, and shy in social relationships, as in nursery school, where he relates better to the teacher than to the other children.

EMOTIONS

In this respect as in others, unless we know our own child well and know what it is reasonable to expect of him and what his behavior really means, we are apt to misjudge him. It is important for parents to know that the typical *endomorph* expresses his emotions fully and freely. He may cry as if his heart will break, but then gets over it quickly. He is easily comforted with kisses and hugs. Loud howls do not necessarily mean that he is in great difficulty.

The *ectomorph*, even as a very young child, finds it much harder to express his emotions. He may suffer deeply without shedding a tear. Parents and teachers need to keep an eye on him, since it may be hard for him to show when he is in trouble. If he does break down and cry, especially in nursery school or day care, it may embarrass him deeply. It is difficult to comfort him because it is hard for him to accept physical comforting.

He is the child who minds terribly if he does not get his "turn," but may find it extremely difficult to *ask* for a turn. He needs more help and support emotionally than do other children.

Things are quite different with the *mesomorph*, who may be characterized as one whose emotions are best expressed in his love of power. He loves to compete, to dominate, to command, to conquer. He has great push, drive, and energy. He is *not* sensitive to the feelings of others, and seems himself almost insensitive to pain. He is courageous and likes to lead. If angry or upset, he tends to take it out on somebody, usually his mother or a younger sibling.

PROBLEMS

Here are some of the things that cause parents the most anxiety about behaviors characteristic of children of different body types:

The *endomorph*, typically jolly, friendly, and well adjusted, does not, as a rule, pose any great problem to his parents. As a baby, such a child is often described as unusually "good." He eats well, sleeps well, and seems to love life. As he grows older, he gets on well with most everybody. He is a nice kind of child to have around.

If parents, too, are of this temperament, there is not much to worry about. But if parents are more ambitious, then they do tend to worry that their endomorphic child does not try hard enough, does not compete. They consider him lazy, and even in the preschool years his lack of drive may cause them (not him) anxiety. Try to accept the fact that great drive and extreme good nature seldom go hand in hand.

The *mesomorph*, on the other hand, especially in the preschool years before he learns to channel his great energy into acceptable lines, can be a great source of anxiety to his parents. He tends to be constantly active, into everything, highly destructive. His hands must touch everything he sees, and he seems to break nearly everything he touches. His mother is worn out just trying to keep up with him, and he easily earns the reputation of being "the worst child in the neighborhood." Though he usually gets on well with contemporaries (he bosses them around and is looked up to as a leader), he tends to lack sensitivity and thus may be hard to reach. One thing that makes him a lot of trouble to adults is that he is so very loud and noisy.

Though this has its good side as well as its bad, all things seem to suggest action to him. A stick is something to pound with, a flower is something to pick or smell. He may even activate his nouns and say, "It's winding outside." The onrush and speed of his thinking may make him go through periods of mumbling hesitancy, which is not the same as stuttering.

He loves action words: "crash," "bang," "boom." He early and accurately knows the position of things in space. Kinesthetically he feels the positions of on, under, and behind. But it is hard for him to stop and think, for he wants to translate everything into immediate action. He tends to be very speedy, shifts quickly and easily from one activity to another, and does not like to be required to slow down and repeat.

He needs much opportunity for active play, especially outdoor play. He needs somebody strong and tireless to play with him. He needs adults who enjoy rather than suffer from his displays of boundless energy.

The *ectomorph* causes anxiety for quite another reason. He is likely to suffer feeding disturbances and also often has sleeping problems. He may have more than his share of allergies. What worries parents most, however, is his oversensitivity, his social shyness, his immaturity, and the fact that he may not seem to need people. All these things combine to make it hard for him to make friends. Keep in mind that this kind of child needs time alone. He needs people who understand his quietness and shyness. He especially needs parents who will not push him into athletic and social activities for which he may be unsuited.

UNDERSTANDING YOUR CHILD FOR WHAT HE IS

If you have been blessed with an *endomorph*, try to enjoy his warmth and friendliness. Don't push him too hard. He may never be a real go-getter, but if you can accept him for what he is, you and he will both be happy.

With your energetic, trouble-prone *mesomorph*, since spanking and corporal punishment may have only momentary effect, concentrate more on supervision and on providing legitimate outlets for his boundless energy. Try not to "see" everything that happens. You cannot punish him for every "bad" thing he does—there will be too many. Praise him for the good things he does in order to encourage him to repeat them.

Try to keep your equilibrium, protect your property and your child from physical harm, and see that you have some relief every day (school or baby-sitter). Keep in mind that the mesomorphic drive that makes so much trouble now may in later life lead him to great success.

Get as many secure locks as possible to protect medicine and any other dangerous or fragile items in your house. Put other things as high as possible. Give this child a good supply of things to be messy with—clay, dough, paint, sand, water, soap. Also, provide as much equipment as possible for the outlet of gross motor energy—a Jungle Gym, bouncing board, doorway swing.

And now for the *ectomorph*. How can you best help him? One thing is to keep in mind that this boy or girl, though often quite bright, matures slowly. Don't worry about this or about his lack of social success. Later on he may catch up with, or even surpass, in some ways, those who got an earlier start. But most of all, and this is especially important for fathers, let this kind of child know that you like him and appreciate him even if he is not athletic and outgoing, even if he is diffident and shy, even if very small things that go wrong seem to bother him unduly.

A special warning about body types. In trying to figure out your own child's physical type, it is important for you to remember that people are not *all* one thing or another, but rather are a *mixture* of all three components described. It is just that unless a child is unusually well balanced, one component or the other (endomorphy, mesomorphy, or ectomorphy) tends to predominate and in all likelihood will have the most influence on what he will be like.

A further warning about the importance of appreciating the effects of the interaction between heredity (or, in this instance, basic body type) and environment is probably necessary. This is so because many people mistakenly interpret both the Sheldon and the Gesell points of view as ignoring the effect of the environment on the human organism.

Dr. Arnold Gesell first gave this warning back in 1940 when he stated explicitly:

In appraising growth characteristics we must not ignore environmental influences—cultural milieu, siblings, parents, food, illness, trauma, education. But these must always be considered in relation to primary or constitutional factors, because the latter ultimately determine the degree, and even the mode of reaction to the environment. The organism always participates in the creation of its environment, and the growth characteristics of the child are really the end-product expressions of an *interaction* between intrinsic and extrinsic determiners. Because the *interaction* is the crux, the distinction between these two sets of determiners should not be too heavily drawn.[6]

SENSE OF SELF

One extremely important part of any child's individuality, and one about which adults are becoming increasingly concerned, is his sense of self or the way he feels about himself. Parental emphasis is shifting, somewhat, from interest in the child's accomplishments—having him do the "right" thing—to his feelings about himself as a person.

Clearly, two of the best ways to make a child feel good about himself are to let him know that you like him—that he pleases you—and to help see to it that much of the time he encounters situations in which he can perform successfully.

The better you understand your child as a person, with all his strong points and his weak ones, the more effectively you can manage to see that much of the time he will be successful.

It is here that a good understanding of the child's physical body, and how that body may in general be expected to behave, can be so useful. If you have a fairly good understanding of what is and is not reasonable to expect of your child in the way of behavior, it will help you do a better job of letting him be his best self and not trying to twist him out of shape in an effort to have him accomplish the impossible. You can help him to be a good person of his own kind without trying to make him into something he can never be.

As you read our descriptions of the endomorph, mesomorph, and ectomorph you will perhaps appreciate the fruitlessness of trying to change an ectomorph into an endomorph, or an endomorph into mesomorph. And having understood your child *yourself* during his formative years, hopefully you may, when he grows older, help him to understand *himself*.

But a person's very physical structure will to some extent limit the extent to which he will, early or late, take an interest in his own individuality. The typical mesomorph acts—without too much introspection. The typical endomorph feels—without perhaps worrying too much about his own self or his own personality. It is the sensitive ectomorph who perhaps is most concerned about and most interested in his own individuality, in himself as a person. Even in this respect children vary, and every child is an individual.

chapter nine
STORIES FROM REAL LIFE

MOTHER CAN'T STAND HER FOUR-YEAR-OLD

Dear Doctors:

When I was a teenager I remember reading something about how wild Four-year-olds are. Little did I realize that in just a few years I would be the mother of one of these little monsters.

Our daughter Sandy is terribly fresh, rude, hard to manage. She seems to accept no limits. Sometimes she exasperates me to the point of active dislike. She is bright and affectionate with others and is no bother when visiting. But in our house I can't stand her positive manner and her insistence on always having her own way. She loves lipstick and dressing up in adult clothes. How I hate to hear her clumping around in those shoes!

For a while we sent her to nursery school because I couldn't cope with her. Fortunately she does get on well with her dad. I would appreciate any suggestions as she is really spoiling my life to the point of quiet desperation.

Your very best bet in calming down any Four-year-old's wilder ways is to ignore them as much as you possibly can. At least some of their wildness is to attract attention, and if nobody cares, what's the fun?

An opposite technique is that, if your daughter is being exaggerated and silly, you go even farther in exaggeration and silliness. She will love it, and you may both have fun.

You say that Sandy will accept no limits. Have you tried specific directions: "as far as the gate," "when the big hand on the clock is at the top," "It's the rule that you mustn't throw toys"? Many will accept such directions. Or, in a more positive vein, try going along with Four's love of newness and adventure. Take your daughter on trips, take her on excursions, especially since you say she is good when visiting.

Take advantage of the Four-year-old's love of praise. Find something to praise Sandy for, and praise her lavishly. Take advantage of the child's love of "tricks" and new ways of doing things to liven up your daily routines.

There are many little girls, like Sandy, whose lives, at Four, seem to be spent in dress-up dresses, walking around in high-heeled shoes, or wearing old lace curtains, wanting to wear fingernail polish and even lipstick. This kind of play is pretty tiresome to watch, but if it can be used in a dramatic way, it can be contained within rather specific time intervals; and if you can bring yourself to take part, it can be less wearing for you and more fun for her. Have a box of special clothes and a special time for dressing up.

Since Sandy gets on well with her father, try to persuade him to take her for occasional Saturday or Sunday excursions. Even short periods when you are completely free of her presence can do a lot toward giving you a better attitude toward your demanding daughter.

We don't blame any mother for feeling at least temporary dislike for some one of her children. But remember, *you are the only mother she has.* For her to feel that certain of her specific behaviors annoy you, and won't be permitted, is reasonable. But it would be pretty tragic for her if she believed that you really did not like her.

FOUR-YEAR-OLDS DON'T ALWAYS TELL THE TRUTH

Dear Doctors:

I am very much concerned about my Four-year-old son, our first and so far our only child. My wife and I are churchgoing people, and we have very strong standards of right and wrong. We have always impressed on Irwin the importance of telling the truth.

But the other day, when my wife caught him misbehaving, within the first five minutes of questioning he had five different lies about what had actually happened. Where and how did we go wrong? How can we impress on Irwin that he must tell the truth?

You can impress on Irwin that he must tell the truth by continuing as you have begun. Maintain your own firm standards of right and wrong, set a good example for him, and, when the occasion arises, emphasize to him the importance of truth.

And then you wait. The majority of Four-year-olds do not always tell the truth. Four is a time when children boast and brag and exaggerate, and, above all, lie. No matter how good your example or your teaching, most Fours are not ready to tell all of the truth all of the time.

Our guess is that both you and your wife perhaps need to know much more than you do about how normal children develop.

THERE'S NOTHING WRONG WITH HAVING AN IMAGINARY COMPANION

Dear Doctors:

My husband and I are the somewhat older parents of an only child, a Four-year-old boy named Jonathan. He has been a delight to us, and we try to be good parents, though sometimes we feel we don't know as much as we should about children.

Only one aspect of his behavior troubles us, and has

done so for the past eight months. Though Jonathan has plenty of friends to play with in the neighborhood, he devotes most of his time, and his interest, to a purely imaginary playmate named Tulipka. Tulipka not only takes up vast amounts of his time, but she rules our household.

If Tulipka won't go on a walk or auto ride, Jonathan won't go, either. If Tulipka doesn't like a certain food, Jonathan won't eat it, either. Etc. This goes on all day long, every day.

Our friends and our pediatrician give widely differing advice about this strange phenomenon. This varies as follows:

a) The behavior is normal,

b) It is a sign that Jonathan is emotionally disturbed since he can't distinguish reality from unreality,

c) Jonathan plays this way because he is an only child and thus lonely. Some feel we should permit the behavior, or even encourage it; others say we should stop it. Can you advise?

We vote for (a); that is, we believe the behavior is normal. It is by no means a sign that Jonathan is lonely, but rather suggests that he is a highly imaginative and probably intelligent youngster who is clinging, a bit long and hard, to an extremely typical Three-and-a-half-year-old kind of behavior. Some of the most superior boys and girls that we have known do enjoy their imaginary companions.

We can practically guarantee that the behavior will drop out, or most certainly diminish, within the next few months. In the meantime, take advantage of it while it lasts. If you want him to do something, tell him—quickly, before Tulipka has a chance to object—that Tulipka does this particular thing so nicely. Or, suggest that "You and Tulipka might like to come out for a nice walk." Use her as an ally, not an enemy. And don't worry.

BABY-SITTER, TIME WITH DAD, SUGGESTED AS SOLUTIONS
TO WHINING PROBLEM

Dear Doctors:

My problem, in one word, is whining!

Jacob is Four and has whined on and off for the last
several months. It was very bad at Three-and-a-half,
dropped off a bit, and now is ten times as bad as ever.

We hoped nursery school would help. It does. But he
goes only three mornings a week, and the days he is
at home are brutal. If I stop my housework and spend
time with him, he is fine for ten minutes. Then he says,
"Go back to your ironing, Mommy." But then the whining starts again.

Unfortunately, I don't have a car, so can't take him
with me shopping and visiting, which he loves. He has
no other tensional outlet except whining.

Possibly whining has driven more mothers over the brink
than anything else. Fortunately, it seems to come and go
with Jacob. You can hope for an improvement by Five.

In the meantime, we think you'll have to plan your
days, when he isn't in nursery school, with a little more
time with Jacob and a little less with housework.

You say you haven't a car, but surely there are short
excursions near home that you can arrange to satisfy him.
A very small thing makes a big excursion for a little boy.
Just to watch some excavation; a short trip to some
neighborhood store; whatever your neighborhood offers.

You say he is sociable, and most Fours love to visit. Do
you have any neighbors who would receive him for a
short visit if you planned it with them?

Also, we think that Jacob would be less likely to whine
with a baby-sitter than with you. Could you plan, say, two
afternoons a week after his nap, to have somebody come
and take him out for an hour or two?

Tired children tend to whine most at the end of the day
when you are getting dinner. Possibly you could have the

sitter come late instead of early. Or, perhaps you could arrange to feed Jacob early and get him to bed before that bad five-to-seven-o'clock hour when everybody in the family is likely to be at his worst.

All of this planning is not guaranteed to make your son less whiny. But he is *much less likely* to whine when he is rather fully occupied. On weekends we hope his father can take a turn. Most boys don't whine when they're out alone with their fathers.

FOUR-YEAR-OLD WON'T EAT

Dear Doctors:

I have three children, a girl of Six and two boys— a Four-year-old and one who is ten months old. The Four-year-old boy presents all my problems. He refuses to eat. Last year we brought him to a doctor for a checkup as he was always complaining of a stomachache at mealtimes. The doctor told us there was nothing wrong with him physically and suggested we ignore him and that he would eat when he got hungry.

Well, for several months we went along with the doctor's suggestion, ignoring his threats of "I'm not eating tonight." He ate just what he liked—salad and desserts. This method of ignoring him did not help. Really, he eats almost nothing! I believe it only shrank his stomach up. He still wouldn't eat the proper foods.

So, back to the old routine of forcing him, bribing, punishing.

Does every mother have to go through this? My girl never presented this problem. Please tell me what you suggest as we are getting so we dread mealtime with him around. He will eat when he visits his aunt and we're not there. We can't let him starve to death. Can you suggest some method we haven't tried?

We'd like to answer in the words of another mother who had your same problem. Here is what she suggests:

1. The hardest part is for the mother and dad to change

their attitude. I myself used to feel desperate, too. After you've checked with your doctor that your child is healthy even though he doesn't eat much, accept it.

2. Don't keep any sweets around. Exclude them entirely except for birthdays. We used to wait for our dessert and coffee until our three boys were in bed.

3. Unless it is much more convenient to serve him alone, feed your noneater with the family. I used to feel far worse when I had especially prepared something for the little darling and then he didn't eat it.

4. Give the small eater only a half teaspoon of everything and say nothing. Be prepared to scrape the plate into the garbage for quite a while.

5. Don't you two sit there eating and watching him. Plan your conversation ahead of time if you must so you can keep it going easily.

6. Excuse him with a smile even if he has only just arrived at the table, if he wants to get down.

7. We didn't let our boys help themselves because they think dishing up is great fun but usually can't eat as much as they take. This same thing often applies to choosing their own menus. It may work out to let them choose between two kinds of fruit or two kinds of vegetable. Complete freedom of choice often ends up with difficult or peculiar menus, which they may not eat even after they have chosen them.

8. Between-meal snacks seem to be an individual matter. Our boys ate just as much, or rather as little, for meals whether they had them or not, so we allowed nourishing snacks. Raisins, fruit juices, and crackers were favorites.

9. A few foods you may not have tried yet for snacks or part of the meal: one or two dried prunes or figs; a small amount of grated American cheese; an egg beaten up in orange juice, or in milk with vanilla and sugar. Serve only half a glassful, with a colored straw. Popcorn made at home is good, also quartered apples.

10. The most important thing is to realize what a very *small* appetite many children have.

GIRL PULLS COVERS OVER HEAD AT BEDTIME

Dear Doctors:

I have read your writings for several years and marvel at your solutions for people who seem to need them. I hope you can do the same for me.

I have what I think is a problem with my Four-and-a-half-year-old daughter Martha. It just started recently. When she goes to sleep at night she has to have her head covered up, no matter what the weather.

If she sleeps with someone else, or takes her nap in the daytime, she doesn't cover her head. Just at night if she is alone. I have talked with her, warned her that she may smother, even spanked her, but it does no good. She waits until she thinks everyone is asleep and then covers her head. I've asked her if she is afraid of something, but she says no.

Is this just a stage? If not, how can I stop her?

Martha's rather odd bedtime behavior is probably just a stage, though admittedly you don't want her to smother while she is going through this stage.

Actually your daughter is solving her Four-year-old problem rather nicely. She is just blotting out all visual stimuli. This is a stage when many children are very much aware of shadows or of moving lights. Even figured wallpaper may seem to move. Sometimes they are awakened when car lights suddenly flash through their window.

When a child has this trouble of adjusting to light and shadows, we are cautious about where her bed is placed in the room, so that she isn't looking into the window. Or, shades can keep out light stimuli. But then the darkness may be too intense, so that you may wish to relieve it by a baseboard low-voltage light that will not cast shadows. Or, leave the door ajar into the hall, where a light may be kept on.

You may be able to purchase one of those little phosphorescent figures or pictures that many children love.

These give off light and also give a feeling of companionship.

We have never heard of a child suffocating when she chose to keep the covers over her head, though parents may feel more comfortable if she uses one of the more porous blankets. But we would recommend trying to find out just why your daughter does this. The presence of another person seems to dispel her fears, which suggests that they are not too deep-seated.

REASSURANCE, STORYTELLING MAY HELP CHILD FRIGHTENED BY NIGHTMARES

Dear Doctors:

My Four-and-a-half-year-old daughter Andrea has been waking up about an hour after she gets to sleep, with nightmares. She cries, trembles, pulls at her bangs, and seems terribly nervous and upset. Her speech is incoherent, and she has difficulty telling me what's the matter.

Last night she was asking me, "Where is Andrea?" I explained to her that she was Andrea. I can usually quiet her, but often she just gets to sleep and then goes through the whole thing again. She thinks bugs are crawling in her bed.

Our doctor prescribed a nerve tonic, but it hasn't helped too much. During the day she is fine. She is devoted to her twin brother and plays well with him and with a younger sister, though she won't stand up for herself. Rather, in any quarrel, she throws herself on the floor and cries.

It may be that I'm making too much of this, but I would appreciate an opinion.

Nightmares are common to Four-year-olds. We doubt that anything is seriously wrong, but it is disquieting. Andrea may need to build up a little more stamina in playing with her siblings, but her nightmares are not unusual for a girl of this age. And they may continue for the next several years.

Her frightened, bewildered manner naturally frightens you. But about all you can do—aside from trying to see that her days are happy, well filled, and not too demanding or exciting—is what you have been doing. Comfort her, soothe her, talk to her, and then put her back to bed.

Some children are soothed at such times by a little food or drink, or by washing their faces with cold water. Taking them out of their bed and into other surroundings often helps.

As to the bugs and things in her room and bed, these, too, are quite common. Some parents do best by assuring the child that there aren't really any bugs. Others get best results by shooing wild beasts away, brushing the bugs out of the bed, either with their hand or with a whisk broom. Andrea might like and might benefit by hearing a very good bedtime book called *Bedtime for Frances*, by Russell Hoban.

Thus, from a practical point of view, about all you can do is continue what you have been doing. See that she has a nice, relaxed, cozy bedtime period, with reading from her favorite books, the usual kissing and goodnight wishes along with her prayers.

However, don't forget that all fear is not necessarily unpleasant to children. One little Three-and-a-half-year-old we know told us one day that he was afraid of everything, "even my own name." He added, "Major [his dog] scares me. Even dreams scare me." He reported with satisfaction that alligators sometimes bit him in his dreams.

At any rate, nightmares at Four are natural and probably harmless, even though possibly a little unsettling to all concerned.

MOTHER HAS FOUR WET CHILDREN

Dear Doctors:

Like the "bed-wetting family" you wrote about recently, I have four wet children. I resigned myself to letting them grow out of it, thinking it was common. But is it?

My biggest problem right now is my Four-year-old girl Tammy. She still wets at night, but like the others she at least would wear rubber pants, which kept the bed fairly dry. However, the other day she ran outdoors the first thing. A Five-year-old neighbor saw the rubber pants and taunted her, "Baby pants! Baby pants!" That did it.

Since then she won't wear rubber pants, just diapers. So, each night she wets right through her diaper and floods the bed. I had never thought too much about the whole thing before. But I began to wonder. So I conducted a neighborhood survey of thirty families with forty-one kids past Three years.

Here's what I found: Twenty-nine were dry at night as early as Three years of age; thirty-eight were dry by Three-and-a-half; forty of the forty-one were dry at night by Four years.

Yet, all the stores sell the Four-year-old size of rubber pants. Either my own children are unusual, or most parents are ashamed to admit the truth, even in this enlightened day. Can you tell me where to get accurate information about the percentage of Four-year-olds who are not yet dry?

We doubt that the percentages you ask for are available. However, a parent would be insecure indeed if she needed percentages to convince her of the simple and generally accepted fact that it is not unusual for a Four-year-old to be wet at night.

As to the figures you gathered, either the forty-one children in your neighborhood are unusual, or their mothers are less than truthful. It is not at all unusual for Three-year-olds, Four-year-olds, Five-year-olds, and even Six-year-olds to be wet at night. Rubber pants for Four-year-olds are available because they sell. We receive more letters asking how to dry up Four- and Five- and Six-year-olds than any other single question asked.

We assume that you do use a rubber sheet on Tammy's bed. Could you get her to go back to rubber pants by providing shortie nightgowns with matching pants but telling her that she can't have the matching pants unless she wears her rubber pants underneath? You may easily have a year or more to go, and that would be a lot of wet beds.

How old are your other three bed-wetting children? If they are younger, you have your hands full. If they are older, you'd better think of using one of the conditioning devices mentioned in the following letter.

CONDITIONING DEVICE MAY HELP OLDER BED WETTERS

Dear Doctors:

I read in the paper about a mother who made her Five-year-old son stay in his room and do without food because he wet his bed. I have a Four-year-old girl who also wet the bed until I found a product to help her.

I called in about an ad in the paper about bed wetting. Believe me, it was out of this world to rent ($300 a month, with a year's guarantee). In thirty days the child is supposed to have stopped. However, I was then told that one of the department stores had a similar device. I called and found out that they put one out for under $50. It is battery operated with two tinfoil sheets and a separating pad. A buzzer sounds as the child starts wetting. (The tinfoil sheets can be replaced very cheaply if necessary.)

More people should be informed about this. I used it on my daughter, and three weeks to the day she was broken of wetting her bed. I also showed this to my doctor, who had never heard of it. I now have ours stored in our cupboard, should we ever need it again.

I wish more people knew about this product. It would help lots of bed wetters because the buzzer rings until the person gets up and shuts it off.

We are glad to quote your letter because we believe that your experience may be helpful to many who face this problem of bedwetting and do not already know about the several excellent conditioning devices now on the market.

There has, unfortunately, been a school of psychological and medical thought that holds that bedwetting is a sign of emotional disturbance, and that since it is a symptom of trouble, if you clear up the symptom, you still have the trouble.

Now it is certainly possible that a child who is emotionally disturbed may, among other difficulties, be a bed wetter. But we know of no evidence to prove that all bed wetters are emotionally disturbed or that emotional disturbance necessarily has anything to do with bedwetting. It has been our experience that some children are just naturally late in attaining dryness, just as others talk late or walk late.

Age is generally the biggest problem solver when there is late wetness. Thus, we ourselves prefer to wait until a child is at least Six (preferably Seven) before stepping in with outside help, such as the kind of device that this mother mentions. By Six or Seven, however, many parents do find that even a week or two with one of these mechanical devices will bring about the desired dryness.

With a few children who are thus dried up, there may be a relapse, and the conditioning device must again be resorted to. With others, the dryness, once achieved, is permanent.

These conditioning devices come in all prices, so it is easy for any family to pick out one they can afford. It is best to use them under the guidance of your own pediatrician if you are fortunate enough to have one who approves of them. Our favorite of these devices is called WET-NO-MORE, sold by Travis International Inc. of Coos Bay, Oregon, phone (503) 269-6969.

DIFFICULT TO STOP THUMB SUCKING IN EARLY YEARS

Dear Doctors:

My Four-year-old daughter Donna constantly sucks her thumb. My dentist recommends that she stop this habit now. Is there any advice you can give me about this problem? Or, better yet, do you know of any device I may use to help my child correct this habit?

Some dentists do indeed take a very dim view of thumb sucking. But most today seem to believe that if sucking of an intense nature stops before the second teeth come in, probably little harm will be done if Nature has lined the teeth up straight to begin with.

Our own preference is not to make too much of the whole thing, certainly in the years before Six or so. Most children realize that their parents do not especially favor this behavior. Many by Five or Six are old enough to accept the rule that if they want to suck their thumb, they must go into their own room to do it.

Earlier, how much effort you make to stop the sucking can best be determined by the extensity and intensity of the behavior. If you have a child who sucks much of the day and most of the night, chances are your efforts to terminate the behavior will not be effective. And if you talk too much about it too soon, the child will become deaf to the sound of your voice later on when you might otherwise have had a chance.

Yes, there are devices, rather horrible-looking little wire devices, which can be fastened to the roof of the child's mouth and which then scratch the thumb as the child sucks. We have never recommended these, but your doctor might provide one if you wish.

Our own feeling is that if the child needs the comfort of his thumb, perhaps he's lucky that nature provided this handy device for consoling oneself. Most children no longer suck much in the daytime after they start school.

If sucking does persist on into the school years, then

the child may be old enough to plan with you for ways that will help him give up his habit. Four is not, in our opinion, a very good age to make an issue, but it can be an age when a child often restricts sucking to going to sleep. This suggests it is on its way out.

Many mothers now call thumb sucking a *tensional outlet* rather than a *bad habit*, and are not hostile to it. And there is now available a very comforting little book called *Danny and His Thumb*, by Kathryn Ernst, which actually goes so far as to assure young thumb suckers that their behavior is all right and urges them not to worry about it.

HOW TO TELL BOY ABOUT NEW BABY

Dear Doctors:

Our Four-year-old son Kenny has been the only one so far. Now we are expecting a baby. Though I am already six months pregnant, Kenny hasn't seemed to notice anything different about me. I am wondering when I should tell him about the coming addition to the family and what I should tell him.

How to tell him? In as unembarrassed and straightforward and matter-of-fact a way as you can manage.

What to tell him? Well, you know the facts. His own questions, once you have brought up the subject, will give you clues as to just what kind of information he is ready for. Some Four-year-olds are ready to believe that the baby grows inside their mother, but others cling to their earlier notion that it is purchased. Tell Kenneth the truth, but don't belabor the issue, and if he doesn't want to believe, don't insist.

When to tell him? You have done well, especially since he hasn't asked any questions, to delay telling him as long as you have. Four-year-olds have a quite different time sense from our own, and when a mother gives this information at the very beginning of her pregnancy, any preschooler grows very tired of waiting for the blessed event.

Any one of the many good books now on the market can help Kenny understand what it is you are talking about. If it's not too frank for you, we strongly recommend *Where Did I Come From?*, by Peter Mayle. If you want something more conservative, try *The Baby House*, by Norma Simon, *Before You Were a Baby*, by Paul and Kay Showers, or *Making Babies*, by Sara Bonnett Stein.

FOUR-YEAR-OLD MASTURBATES

Dear Doctors:

Our little boy, who is just Four years old, has been masturbating since the age of seven months. His only sibling is an Eleven-year-old sister with whom relations are exceptionally good. But otherwise he is a lonesome little fellow. We live in a third-floor apartment, with the people under us objecting to noise. And I can't allow him to play in the street with other children, who are invariably unattended.

Ours is a reasonably happy and well-adjusted home, and both our children are loved and wanted. The masturbating has increased lately, and there doesn't seem to be anything we can do to restrain him. We tried additional expressions of love, we tried to divert his attention, and we tried spanking and even a "serious talk." Nothing helps because, as he insists tearfully, "I have to do it so I'll feel better." We would greatly appreciate advice.

When a child masturbates during the first year of life, the course of this behavior may be a fairly long one.

You have tried all sorts of diverting techniques, but the problem continues. In general, Four and Six years of age are periods when boys, especially, have increased genital sensations and often do grasp their genitals. Your son's tension sensations may be more marked than they will later on.

In the same way you'd handle thumb sucking, you can at least request that he go into his room to indulge in this

125

behavior and not do it in the presence of other people. Unquestionably, better outlets, such as a good play group, nursery school, or time outdoors with you (going for walks and excursions) would help considerably.

The very fact that he knows what he is doing makes us feel it is not just an automatic release. He sounds like a boy who a little later will really try to stop.

Few if any child specialists know how to stop this behavior, and many think it may be best not to step in at all. Except for the hygienic aspect, many feel that masturbation does not harm children unless they do it excessively. Your son's behavior does seem a little excessive, and hopefully more outside interests will make it unnecessary for him to rely on himself quite so much. So, for the present, try to work up good play interests for your boy, with more attention from both you and his father.

Eventually, if the problem continues into school age and interferes with school adjustment, you may need to take him to a local child guidance clinic for professional help. In the meantime, *must* you continue to live in a third-floor apartment? If there is any way to make your home environment more relaxed it might be of great help to your son.

SEX PLAY

Dear Doctors:

My Four-year-old Jennie and her friend David, who is Five, play together a good deal. About two years ago they began undressing and going to the bathroom outside. David's mother and I tried to stop this by explanations to the youngsters, and by watching them more closely. Last year, more tricks were added to this fascinating game. Again, I spoke to David's mother, and I personally kept them under closer supervision. David delights in a closed door or a secret hiding place. To be honest, Jennie also seems to enjoy this sort of thing.

Last week I returned home to find Jennie and David in her bedroom behind a closed door, again with their pants at half mast. My husband was at home but paid little attention to them as long as they were playing quietly. He feels I'm making too much of this. David's mother, too, seems quite satisfied to leave them to their own devices. Am I right to worry?

Your problem is a common one, and opinions differ. Some child specialists do not think sex play is particularly harmful at the younger ages, and believe that too much suppression and scolding might harm a child more than the actual play itself.

Most mothers don't like it and do prefer to prevent it. (Fathers are more unpredictable. They tend either to get very angry or to be quite indifferent.) So far as we know, adequate supervision is about the only way to prevent it. Talking, scolding, and punishing don't do much good. If the interest is there, and the opportunity presents itself, sex play does take place. If David and Jennie are going to play together, you will just have to supervise very closely.

Sometimes it is hard to supervise directly. But try to have them play in clear and open areas. Avoid closed doors and small, isolated places and bedrooms. Then, if the behavior still continues, the children may have to be separated for a few weeks. This may get the message across.

We're glad you recognize that, enthusiastic as David may be about all this, Jennie is also enthusiastic. Sometimes the greatest harm that comes from neighborhood sex play is that all the mothers of children involved become angry at each other and blame each others' children. It is important for all mothers to appreciate that this kind of play goes on in "good" neighborhoods as well as in "bad"; among "nice" children as well as among "naughty" ones.

Here are a few general comments on the subject:

Circumstances have a lot to do with it. There are some children who might skip it altogether if they never got a chance to play alone without supervision, or were always extremely busy at more productive activity. It is much worse in some children than in others; worse at some ages than at others.

Probably the two main things to do about it are: First, be calm and casual. Give the child the impression that you don't favor (or won't permit) this kind of thing. But avoid being shocked, horrified, or overly upset. The harm you might do a child by your attitude that sex activity is wrong and awful and shameful might do much greater damage than the actual sex play itself.

Second, try to keep your child out of situations that will lead to sex play. Some playmates may seem to arouse this more than others. There may be periods when you will avoid having him or her play with just those children. Or, there will be times when your child, in certain combinations, just can't seem to play unsupervised without getting into such activity.

A rather extreme but workable solution is to get one-piece underwear and also one-piece playsuits except for dress-up. Mere inaccessibility *can* provide an answer.

Who is to *blame* isn't the important thing. The boy next door may start it this year; next year it may be your own child who makes the initiating moves. We don't say that sex play is universal, but it seems to be nearly so. The absence of any sex interest or questions may be more indicative of later difficulties than a too great early interest.

BOY SUDDENLY AFRAID OF DYING

Dear Doctors:

Our Four-and-a-half-year-old son Robby has all of a sudden become terrified at the idea of dying. He had a pet dog die about a year ago, and we thought he had a general notion of the whole thing.

But now, all of a sudden, he is so frightened. My

wife assured him that nobody in this family was going to die. I thought that was wrong because she couldn't guarantee it. So I told him about God and that if he or any of us did die, we would go to be with God, so we would be all right.

Now he seems more frightened than ever because he says he doesn't *want* to go to be with God. What do we do now? His worry seems to be specifically about himself, and that he himself will die.

There are ages when the thought of God *can* bring children comfort in certain situations. The thought of God as a Father who takes care of you can sometimes allay the fears of a Four-year-old. But a child of this age has a lot of trouble with himself about what is real and what is not.

As reality takes a stronger hold, Robby may be able to accept the fact that people die mostly when they are old. But most Four-year-olds have only a very limited notion of what death means. You may be amazed at your son's callousness by the time he is Five. Many Five-year-olds in their discussions of death are like little lawyers, investigating the circumstances of death and the position of the body and just what will happen.

Some at Four, and many at Five, tend to think of death as reversible.

But Four-and-a-half-year-olds tend to be great worriers. Even without the impact of a specific experience, anxieties, and especially anxieties about death, do crop up. Some can be helped to an acceptance of the reality of death by the death of a pet. This didn't seem to help with Robby.

The notion of God does help some Four-year-olds, but Robby would probably have been helped more by the notion that God—if you wish to bring in this concept—is protecting him and looking out for him here on earth so that he won't die, rather than that if he went to Heaven he would be with God. Perhaps you can backtrack a little.

What Robby wants right now is a strong assurance that

he himself and, if possible, all members of his immediate family are going to be all right. Even though life is at best uncertain, we do think you would be reasonably safe to give him the assurance he seeks. However, word it a little loosely, so that you can get out of it if disaster should strike somebody near or dear.

HOW DO YOU TELL A FOUR-YEAR-OLD ABOUT DIVORCE?

Dear Doctors:

I am very much concerned about something that is happening in our family and don't know how to handle it. My husband and I are getting a divorce, and so far we haven't broken this news to our Four-year-old son Jimmy. How can I tell him? How will he take it? Do you think the effects of divorce are always disastrous to a young child?

My husband and I have known for some time that our marriage was not working out. At first we hoped we could manage to stay together for Jimmy's sake. Now we know that isn't possible. Help!

We think you are right *not* to stay together "for the sake of your son." Child specialists have long felt that it is the emotional divorce that precedes the legal divorce that harms most.

Jimmy, obviously, will not welcome this news. Even a young child generally would prefer that his family, even though an unhappy one, remain intact. However, a very young child often recovers from divorce, and adapts to a new way of living, more easily than an older one.

Jimmy will be most influenced, perhaps, by the way you and your husband conduct yourselves. If both of you remain calm, and at least superficially friendly, and you yourself don't act as if the end of the world had come, chances are that Jimmy, like thousands of other children of divorce, will survive emotionally.

So, make every effort to convey to your son that what

is happening is not dreadful. Assure him that his father is not leaving because of anything that he, Jimmy, has done or has not done. Assure him that his father will still be his father and that his father still loves him. Tell him specifically that he will continue to see his father.

Do your very best to refrain from saying hostile or ugly things about your husband. Try to give the explanation of why he is leaving in as calm and matter-of-fact a way as you can, explaining that when people marry they hope it will last forever but that sometimes it just doesn't work out that way. This does not mean that either person is bad, or that either does not love the child.

Be sure to emphasize to Jimmy that though his father will no longer be your husband he still will be Jimmy's father and will not be lost to him.

And, from a practical point of view, because even a Four-year-old does have practical questions, tell him what is going to happen to him. Thus, tell him, if this is the case, that he will go right on living in his own house and that he will have a chance to visit with his father on weekends. Parents need to determine the most desirable frequency of visits. Often, once every three or four weeks works out better than the more customary every weekend.

Be aware, too, that with the very young boy or girl you may need to give the same information more than once.

SHOULD YOU TREAT TWINS ALIKE?

Dear Doctors:

My husband and I have Four-year-old girl twins, Jane and Samantha. They are darling little girls, and we have had a reasonably easy time of it so far. Our problem now concerns school this fall. The twins are very close to each other and, though we certainly haven't pushed it, like to do things together. Some of our friends say they should be separated when they go to school. We're afraid that would be extremely upsetting to them both. Should we, or shouldn't we, urge the school to keep them together in kindergarten? And, can you recommend a good book on twinning?

People nowadays seem to feel rather strongly that twins should not be dressed alike, named alike, or kept always together. Most seem to feel that each twin should be treated as much like an individual as possible, even though it is a temptation to make a lot of their twinship.

Thus, it is generally felt that it's best to separate them in school. Then if they want to stick closely together in out-of-school hours, that's up to them. Kindergarten can be an exception. If your girls are the kind who find it hard to accept and adapt to new experiences, you may feel that school in itself will be enough of a problem without facing them with the problem of separating from each other.

If in your judgment they can make it, it would probably be desirable to start them in separate classrooms. If not, you might prefer to have them together in kindergarten and then start the separation with first grade. However, it can make a difference whether twins are identical or fraternal. We tend to allow identical twins to stay together until they are ready to separate. This may not be until third or fourth grade or even considerably later. But the sooner you separate fraternal twins, possibly the better.

The best current book that talks about twins much past infancy is Betty Rothbart's *Multiple Blessings*.

WILL BOY BE BORED IN KINDERGARTEN IF HE GOES TO NURSERY SCHOOL FIRST?

Dear Doctors:

I would like to send my oldest son, now Four, to nursery school. But people tell me that if he goes to nursery school now, he will be bored next year in kindergarten, and even more bored in first grade because by then he will be tired of school. Do you think this is true? And can you explain to me, clearly, the differences between kindergarten and nursery school?

Kindergarten and nursery school are not different by some arbitrary ruling. To some extent even the same materials might be used in the two situations.

Rather, they are different because of the different ages and abilities of the children enrolled, which make necessary quite different curriculums. In fact, the daily schedule and type of experience are actually quite different within the nursery school itself for the different age groups.

Thus, all groups might well play with drawing and painting materials, clay, and blocks, but Two-, Three-, Four-, and Five-year-old groups each play with these materials in an entirely different way. The skilled teacher not only recognizes the different needs of children using the same materials but would be prompted to change or modify materials when this is necessary.

The most important aspects of a school are the teacher and the children. Almost any appropriate materials, with skilled guidance, can enable the child to experience the satisfactions of his age level, and can stimulate him to growth toward the age he is to become. In addition, one important aspect of either nursery school or kindergarten is the satisfaction of being with children of one's own age.

As to the danger of being bored, it would be most unlikely for a rich nursery school experience to cause a child to be bored in a following year with a kindergarten experience that would in many ways be entirely different—different not only because the situation is set up differently, but mostly because the child himself is different. In any event, being bored in school seldom occurs because a child is too smart for his grade or because he has had too much earlier school experience. It usually occurs because a child is noncreative in using opportunities that are almost always available in a well-conceived school situation.

SHOULD DONALD START KINDERGARTEN BEFORE HE TURNS FIVE?

Dear Doctors:

My problem is my oldest son, Donald, now Four. He will be Five on November 13. The cut-off date in our town is December 31, so Donnie is eligible to enter kindergarten when school starts in September. Parents are allowed to use their judgment about keeping a child out of school.

My husband, having started school too early himself, knows that school life can be miserable if you are not physically and emotionally ready to accept it. Friends and relatives, however, think we are being overconscientious and that a problem exists only in our minds.

Both my husband and I would rather that Donnie start next year, rather than start now, fail, and then have to be held back. Another factor which contributes to our confusion is that his two best friends will be sent to school according to schedule. We fear that he would be heartbroken, at first, if he were left behind.

Donnie seems to us like a very bright boy, but he is small and seems immature. Both my husband and I are thoroughly confused about this whole problem. It seems that the more we read, the more we find conflicting opinions.

True, there are conflicting opinions. Our own is that it is the very unusual November boy who is ready to start kindergarten in the September *before* he has had his fifth birthday. A December cut-off date is, in our eyes, inexcusable unless a young or Four-and-a-half-year-old kindergarten group is provided. The ideal cut-off date is September 1 or earlier.

You say that your husband knows from his own experience what a too-early start can do. He is right that it is better to start late, rather than to start early and then repeat.

True, Donnie may feel sad if his friends start school before he does. But it would be a very poor decision to put him into a situation where he may be unhappy and may do poorly for the next twelve years or more just to keep from hurting his feelings now.

EPILOGUE

Yes, Four is indeed wild and wonderful. We hope you will enjoy this age to its full because Five, if growth follows its usual course, is quite something else again.

Four is exuberant; Five is controlled. Four tests the limits; Five conforms. Four delights in seeing how far he can go; Five wants to do what you, his parents, want him to do.

When your boy or girl is only Four, visions of delinquency may dance before your eyes; when he is Five, you may wonder if he or she isn't perhaps a little *too* good.

The rhythm of growth seems at times almost as lawful as that of the tides. Equilibrium—disequilibrium. Expansion—contraction. If you can add respect for what is going on to your natural love and affection for your own preschooler, you will add immeasurably to *your* enjoyment of these early years as well as to his!

APPENDIXES
Good Toys
for Four-Year-Olds

Animals, toy
Balls
Baskets and boxes
Blocks
Boards and sawhorse for seesaw
Boards for balancing and sliding
Board games, simple
Books
Bouncing board
Brushes for painting
Camera (toy)
Cash register (toy)
Chest of drawers, cupboard, doll-size
Clay
Climbing apparatus, as Jungle Gym, Tower Gym, ladders, boxes
Cooking equipment (toy)
Costume box, including pocketbooks, hats, gloves, scarves, jewelry, curtains, shoes
Crayons, large-size
Dishes and cooking utensils
Doctor and nurse kit
Doll bed, carriage, high chair
Dollhouse
Doll clothing with large buttons and buttonholes
Dolls
Doorway gym
Drawing and coloring materials
Easel
Easel paper
Fingerpaints
Fit-together construction toys and Tinkertoys or Lego
Flannel-surfaced boards and pieces of flannel or felt in different shapes and colors
Flashlight
Garden tools, small
Hammer with short handle and heavy head
Hand puppets
Hollow blocks
Housekeeping toys, including broom, vacuum cleaner, dust mop

Jigsaw puzzles
Jump rope
Kegs
Kites
Logs
Magnets
Miniature people or animals
Musical instruments, such as wrist bells, drum, tambourine, castanets, triangle
Nature specimens, such as fish, turtles, salamanders, rabbits, guinea pigs, or plants. (These of course are not really toys.)
Nests of boxes or cans
Packing boxes large and sturdy enough for child to climb on
Paints and easel
Phonograph and records
Pipes for blowing bubbles
Playhouse
Pregummed dots, squares, triangles of colored paper
Punching bag
Ring toss
Rocking horse
Roller skates
Rope and string
Sailboats (toy)

Sand toys, including spoon, sugar scoop, pail, cans, sifter
Sandbox
Sawhorse
Scissors
Scooter
Scrapbook
Screwing toys
Seesaw
Sled
Slide
Small airplanes, automobiles, trucks, boats, trains
Small boards for building, hauling
Stove
Suitcase
Swing, adjustable
Table and chair, child-size
Toy telephone
Train, dump truck, steam shovel large enough for child to ride on
Tricycle
Wagon
Water-play materials
Wheels of all kinds: cars, dump truck, bulldozer, tractors, wheelbarrow
Workbench and vise

Books for
Four-Year-Olds*

Bang, Molly. *Ten, Nine, Eight*. New York: Greenwillow, 1988.

Bemelmanns, Ludwig. *Madeline*. New York: Viking, 1939.

Brown, Margaret Wise. *The Runaway Bunny*. New York: Harper & Row, 1942.

Cole, Joanna. *Bony Legs*. New York: Macmillan, 1984.

DePaola, Tomie. *Pancakes for Breakfast*. New York: Harcourt Brace Jovanovich, Inc., 1978.

Fox, Mem. *Koala Lou*. New York: Harcourt Brace Jovanovich, Inc., 1989.

Freeman, Don. *Corduroy*. New York: Viking, 1968.

Galdone, Paul. *The Gingerbread Boy*. New York: Houghton Mifflin, 1975.

Hazen, Barbara Shook. *Even if I Did Something Awful?* New York: Macmillan, 1981.

Hines, Anna G. *Daddy Makes the Best Spaghetti*. New York: Houghton Mifflin, 1988.

Hoban, Russell. *Bedtime for Frances*. New York: Harper & Row, 1960.

Hoff, Syd. *Danny and the Dinosaur*. New York: Harper & Row, 1968.

---

*The authors acknowledge substantial help with this list from Nancy Dower.

Hogrogian, Nonny. *One Fine Day*. New York: Macmillan, 1971.

Keats, Ezra Jack. *The Snowy Day*. New York: Viking, 1962.

Lionni, Leo. *Swimmy*. New York: Knopf, 1973.

McCloskey, Robert. *Make Way for Ducklings*. New York: Viking, 1941.

————. *Blueberries for Sale*. New York: Viking, 1948.

Marshall, James. *George and Martha*. New York: Houghton Mifflin, 1974.

Mayer, Mercer. *There's a Nightmare in My Closet*. New York: Dial, 1985.

Numeroff, Laura Joffe. *If You Give a Mouse a Cookie*. New York: HarperCollins, 1985.

Pomerantz, Charlotte. *The Piggy in the Puddle*. New York: Macmillan, 1974.

Pryor, Anslie. *Baby Blue Cat and the Dirty Dog Brothers*. New York: Viking, 1987.

Pulushkin, Maria. *Mother, Mother I Want Another*. New York: Crown, 1986.

Scott, Ann Herbert. *On Mothers' Lap*. Houghton Mifflin, 1972.

Slobodidna, Esphyr. *Caps for Sale*. New York: Harper, 1947.

Wadell, Martin and Benson, Patrick. *Owl Babies*. New York: Candlewick/Penguin, 1992.

Wadell, Martin and Firth, Barbara. *Can't You Sleep Little Bear?* New York: Candlewick/Penguin, 1992.

Zolotow, Charlotte. *I Know a Lady*. New York: Greenwillow, 1984.

Books for the Parents
of Four-Year-Olds

Alexander, Terry Pink. *Make Room for Twins*. New York: Bantam Books, 1987.

Ames, Louise Bates. *Parents Ask*. A syndicated newspaper column. New Haven, Conn.: Gesell Institute, 1952–.

———. *What Am I Doing in This Grade?* Rosemont, N.J.: Programs for Education, 1985.

———. *What Do They Mean I'm Difficult?* Rosemont, N.J.: Programs for Education, 1986.

———. *Questions Parents Ask*. New York: Clarkson Potter, 1988.

———. *Developmental Discipline*. Rosemont, N.J.: Programs for Education, 1990.

———. *Why Am I So Noisy? Why Is She So Shy?* Rosemont, N.J.: Programs for Education, 1990.

Ames, Louise Bates, and Chase, Joan Ames. *Don't Push Your Preschooler*, rev. ed. New York: Harper & Row, 1980.

Ames, Louise Bates, and Haber, Carol Chase. *He Hit Me First*. New York: Dembner/Warner, 1982.

Ames, Louise Bates, and Ilg, Frances L. *Your Five-Year-Old: Sunny and Serene*. New York: Delacorte, 1979.

Biller, Henry, and Meredith, Dennis. *Father Power*. New York: McKay, 1974.

Billman, Sam, and Zalk, Sue R. *Expectant Fathers*. New York: Hawthorne Press, 1978.

Brazelton, T. Berry. *Working and Caring*. Reading, Mass.: Addison-Wesley, 1987.

Collier, Herbert. *The Psychology of Twins: A Practical Handbook.* Phoenix, Ariz. 1974.

Comer, James P., and Poussaint, Alvin F. *Black Child Care: How to Bring Up a Healthy Black Child in America.* New York: Simon & Schuster, 1975.

Crook, William G. *Help for the Hyperactive Child.* Jackson, Tenn.: Professional Books, 1990.

Cuthbertson, Joanne, and Schevill, Susie. *Helping Your Child Sleep Through the Night.* New York: Doubleday, 1985.

Dinkmeyer, Don. *Parent Your Children.* Circle Pines, Minn.: American Guidance Service, 1989.

Dodson, Fitzhugh. *How to Parent.* Los Angeles: Nash, 1970.

———. *How to Father.* Los Angeles: Nash, 1974.

———. *How to Grandparent.* New York: Harper & Row, 1981.

———. *How to Single Parent.* New York: Harper & Row, 1987.

Feingold, Ben. *Why Your Child Is Hyperactive.* New York: Random House, 1975.

Ferber, Richard. *Solve Your Child's Sleep Problems.* New York: Simon & Schuster, 1985.

Galland, Leo. *Superimmunity for Kids.* New York: Dutton, 1988.

Gardner, Richard A. *The Parents' Book About Divorce.* New York: Doubleday, 1977.

———. *The Boys' and Girls' Book About One-Parent Families.* New York: Putnam, 1978.

———. *The Girls' and Boys' Book About Good and Bad Behavior.* Cresskill, N.J.: Creative Therapeutics, 1990.

Gesell, Arnold, et al. *Infant and Child in the Culture of Today,* rev. ed. New York: Harper & Row, 1974.

Goldstein, Sonja, and Solnit, Albert J. *Divorce and Your Child: Practical Suggestions for Parents.* New Haven, Conn.: Yale University Press, 1984.

Graubard, Paul S. *Positive Parenting.* New York: Bobbs Merrill, 1977.

Grollman, Earl A., ed. *Explaining Death to Children.* Boston: Beacon Press, 1967.

Grollman, Earl, and Sweder, Gerri. *The Working Parent Dilemma.* Boston: Beacon Press, 1986.

Harrison-Ross, Phyllis, and Wyden, Barbara. *The Black Child: A Parent's Guide.* New York: Peter Wyden, 1973.

Hatfield, Antoinette, and Stanton, Peggy. *How to Help Your Child Eat Right.* Washington, D.C.: Acropolis Press, 1978.

Ilg, Frances L.; Ames, Louise Bates; and Baker, Sidney M. *Child Behavior,* rev. ed. New York: Harper & Row, 1981.

Kraskin, Robert A. *You Can Improve Your Vision*. New York: Doubleday, 1968.

Lansky, Vicky. *Vicky Lansky's Practical Parenting Tips*. Deephaven, Minn.: Meadowlark Press, 1981.

———. *Vicky Lansky's Divorce Book for Parents*. New York: New American Library, 1989.

Liepmann, Lise. *Your Child's Sensory World*. New York: Dial, 1973.

Marston, Stephanie. *The Magic of Encouragement*. New York: William Morrow, 1990.

Mayle, Peter. *Where Did I Come From?* New York: Lyle Stuart, 1973.

Maynard, Fredelle. *Guiding Your Child to a More Creative Life*. New York: Doubleday, 1973.

Moore, Sheila, and Frost, Roon. *The Little Boy Book*. New York: Clarkson Potter, 1986.

Novello, Joseph R. *How to Survive Your Kids*. New York: McGraw Hill, 1990.

Pitcher, Evelyn G., and Ames, Louise Bates. *The Guidance Nursery School*. New York: Harper & Row, 1975.

Pringle, Lawrence. *Death Is Natural*. New York: Four Winds Press/Morrow, 1990.

Ramos, Suzanne. *The Complete Book of Child Custody*. New York: Putnam, 1978.

Rapp, Doris. *Allergy and the Hyperactive Child*. New York: Sovereign Books, 1984.

Read, Katherine, and Patterson, June. *The Nursery School and Kindergarten*. New York: Holt, Rinchart & Winston, 1980.

Scarr, Sandra. *Mother Care—Other Care*. New York: Basic Books, 1984.

Smith, Lendon. *Feed Your Kids Right*. New York: McGraw Hill, 1979.

Turecki, Stanley. *The Difficult Child*. New York: Bantam, 1989.

——— (with Sarah Wernick). *The Emotional Problems of Normal Children*. New York: Bantam, 1994.

Wood, Chip. *Yardsticks: Children in the Classroom Ages 4 to 12*. Greenfield, Mass.: Northeast Foundation for Children, 1994.

Wunderlich, Ray, and Kalita, Dwight. *Nourishing Your Child*. New Canaan, Conn.: Keats, 1984.

Young, Milton A. *Buttons Are to Push*. New York: Pitman, 1970.

NOTES

1. Information on visual behavior was furnished by Richard J. Apell, O.D., director of the Vision Department of the Gesell Institute of Child Development.
2. In order to make use of a controlled situation, our observations were made during the course of the Gesell Preschool Examination, as described in *The First Five Years of Life,* by Arnold Gesell et al. (New York: Harper & Row, 1940). This examination was given individually to boys and girls of each of the preschool ages.
3. Laurie Braga and Joseph Braga, *Learning and Growing: A Guide to Child Development* (Englewood Cliffs, N.J.: Prentice-Hall, 1975).
4. Among the physicians who have written helpful and informative books on the damaging effects that can come from a harmful diet are Drs. William Crook, Ben J. Feingold, Lendon Smith and Ray Wunderlich, whose books are listed on pages 144 to 146.
5. For a description of these tests see Frances L. Ilg and Louise B. Ames, *School Readiness* (New York: Harper & Row, 1965); and for a discussion of what they mean to the parent, see Louise B. Ames, *Is Your Child in the Wrong Grade?* (New York: Harper & Row, 1967).
6. Arnold Gesell, "Stability of Mental-Growth Careers," *Thirty-ninth Yearbook of the National Society for the Study of Education,* part 2 (Bloomington, Ind.: Public School Publishing Co., 1940).

INDEX

Photo Credits

LOUISE BATES AMES

is a lecturer at the Yale Child Study Center and assistant professor emeritus at Yale University. She is co-founder of the Gesell Institute of Child Development and collaborator or co-author of three dozen of so books, including *The First Five Years of Life*, *Infant and Child in the Culture of Today*, *Child Rorschach Responses*, and the series *Your One-Year-Old* through *Your Ten- to Fourteen-Year-Old*. She has one child, three grandchildren, and four great-grandchildren.

FRANCES L. ILG

wrote numerous books, including *The Child from Five to Ten*, *Youth: The Years from Ten to Sixteen*, and *Child Behavior*, before her death in 1981. She was also a co-founder of the Gesell Institute of Child Development at Yale.